NATIONAL PARKS
OF THE ROCKY MOUNTAINS

NATIONAL PARKS
OF THE ROCKY MOUNTAINS
ROCKY MOUNTAIN · GRAND TETON
YELLOWSTONE · GLACIER/WATERTON LAKES

TEXT
KENT + DONNA DANNEN
PHOTOGRAPHERS
PAUL CHESLEY, JEFF FOOTT,
JAMES FRANK, RON SHADE
AND MANY OTHERS

ROCKY MOUNTAIN NATURE ASSOCIATION
ESTES PARK, COLORADO

Produced by Jürgen F. Boden and Elke Emshoff
Designed by Hartmut Brückner

Published in the United States of America, 1986
by Rocky Mountain Nature Association,
Rocky Mountain National Park,
Estes Park, Colorado 80517

ISBN 0-930487-20-6

Maps of the national parks by permission of Acadia Verlag.

Published simultaneously in the United States of America by Rocky Mountain
Nature Association, Estes Park, Colorado, and in the Federal Republic of Ger-
many, Switzerland, and Austria by Alouette Verlag, Oststeinbek/Hamburg, West
Germany.

Printed and bound in the Federal Republic of Germany by Westermann Druck,
Braunschweig

Cover picture
Bob Paul, park ranger in
Glacier for more than 30
years, paddles his canoe
across Bowman Lake,
reflecting summer
afternoon clouds above
Numa Peak (9,003 feet)
on the left and Rainbow
Peak (9,892 feet).

Acknowledgements

The editors of this book wish to express their gratitude to the many American photographers who so generously submitted their work and time to us. Through their personal interpretations we have been able to present to an international audience this -- so we believe – representative mosaic of life in and around the Rocky Mountains.

Of no lesser importance are the text contributions, which are to fulfill the educational and informational objective of this publication. They have been written with a profound knowledge and a deep feeling for a great region of the North American continent.

We also wish to thank the staffs of Rocky Mountain, Grand Teton, Yellowstone, and Glacier national parks – especially Messrs. Glen Kaye, Pat Smith, George Robinson, and Clyde Lockwood – for their substantial assistance in this endeavor.

Notes on the authors

Kent and *Donna Dannen* are authors of various books about the Rocky Mountain region. Their writing and photography has appeared in most nature-oriented periodicals, as well as on calendars, national television, and various other media. Donna Dannen is a former ranger/naturalist for the National Park Service and has worked as a representative for Eastman Kodak Company, teaching photography in Rocky Mountain National Park. Kent Dannen is a former contributing editor for »Backpacker Magazine.« Both Dannens regularly serve as instructors on a variety of outdoor skill and natural history topics for the National Wildlife Federation Conservation Summit program. They live in Estes Park, Colorado, with their team of Samoyed sled dogs.

Ron Shade grew up in a sparsely populated area of North Central Pennsylvania as the youngest of thirteen children. It was there as a boy that he learned the ways of the white-tailed deer, black bear, wild turkey, and many other animals and birds near his home. While in high school he purchased his first camera and taught himself the techniques of photography.

He then moved to Montana where he served four years in the U.S. Air Force. It wasn't until he took a job in Yellowstone National Park that he looked at photography more seriously, and, under the guidance of the park's photographer Bill Keller, developed his talent to the point where he was able to capture in brilliant pictures what he experienced in the wilderness day by day.

Since then Ron Shade's photographs have been published in numerous books and magazines; he was awarded the Grand Prize in the 1985 National Wildlife Magazine's photo contest. »Photography provides me with an ›excuse‹ for being in the wilderness. I can spend hours and hours watching the wildlife – the photo comes second.«

James Frank is a self-taught photographer who earned a Bachelor of Arts degree in literature and education in a Nebraska college. He moved to Estes Park in 1979 to live in the mountains and develop further his skills by photographing landscapes, flora, and fauna of this rugged region.

He has since photographed extensively in Rocky Mountain National Park and surrounding areas, and expresses a special love and wonder for the tundra landscape and the tenacity of its life forms. »It is a place of tenderness and savage fury, a place of tiny, fragile flowers that may bloom for only a day beside enormous boulders which remain unchanged for centuries. It is a place everyone should experience at least once in his life.«

James Frank has won several awards and his photographs have been published in various brochures, calendars, magazines, and books.

Paul Chesley is a professionally trained photographer whose subjects range from the landscapes and wildlife in the Rocky Mountains to the enigmatic people of Japan; not many photographers are able to disperse their energy among art photography, journalism, and commercial work, but he works well in all these traditionally divergent media.

Based in Aspen, Colorado, Paul Chesley is a regular contributor to the National Geographic's magazines and books; his work has also appeared in numerous other national and international publications. Besides numerous awards, he recently had one-man exhibitions at the Honolulu Academy of Art, the Minneapolis Bell Museum, and the Nishi Ginza Galleries in Tokyo.

Jeff Foott is a man of many skills: he has earned a degree in biology; he has worked as a ranger in Yosemite National Park, as a professional mountain climbing guide in Grand Teton National Park, as a professional ski patrol in Teton Village near Jackson; he is a certified scuba diver, and an expert in kayak and canoe sports.

Jeff Foott also has professional training in still and motion picture photography and is today one of America's celebrated camera-men and directors of nature and wildlife films, and documentaries. His still-life photographs have appeared in literally every nature oriented magazine as well as in numerous books. If he is not traveling, he lives in a small village in Wyoming close to the Teton Range.

Space, unfortunately, does not allow background descriptions on the many other excellent photographers who have contributed their work to this book.

Contents
Text parts

Picture parts

Introduction

The most important completely American contribution to mankind's fund of ideas evolved in the Rocky Mountain West. It was the idea of preserving land in its wild, mostly natural state for the public benefit: the national park idea.

Americans certainly love their national parks – and no less do Canadians. The United States and Canada possess the world's finest collection of these highly revered treasures. National parks do much to help Americans define themselves and their national heritage.

The national parks of the Rocky Mountains – Rocky Mountain, Grand Teton, Yellowstone, and Glacier/Waterton Lakes – are among the oldest, most famous, and most scenic national parks. They are also among the most popular, receiving millions of visitors each year.

Popularity poses a conflict between the two goals of national parks: 1) to preserve the land in its natural state and 2) to permit the public to enjoy the parks and be mentally, physically, morally, and spiritually inspired by them. However, increasingly sophisticated methods of National Park Service management and growing public awareness of the need to use parks delicately have reduced the conflict. Despite an explosion in the number of visitors to national parks in recent decades, the wilderness values of these parks have been preserved and, occasionally, even enhanced.

The difficult balance between use and preservation has been sustained, at least for the present. One of the lessons that national parks themselves teach is that success requires flexibility and adaptability. The public and the National Park Service both will have to become even more flexible and adaptable if national parks are to be optimally used and preserved in the future in order to have this American idea work.

Kent and Donna Dannen

Similarities Among The National Parks

Each national park of the Rocky Mountains has its own unique character and natural history. But Rocky Mountain, Grand Teton, Yellowstone, and Glacier/Waterton Lakes national parks also have much in common. Mountain glaciers have shaped the terrain of each of the national parks in basically the same way, although the final products look somewhat different. And their wild animal and plant populations include many of the same species.

Mountains Carved by Snowflakes

Even though the geological stories of each of the national parks vary considerably, the mountains of them all received their current dramatic outlines from being carved by glaciers. These finishing touches began roughly 3 million years ago with the coming of the Ice Ages. However, identifiable advances of mountain glaciers in the national parks of the Rockies date from only 150,000 years ago. Perhaps action of later glaciers erased signs of earlier glaciers.

When pulses in average high and low temperatures and/or increased precipitation caused more snow to fall in winter than melted in summer, it began to accumulate in glaciers. These formed first on steep slopes below the summits, where wind usually from the west dumped snow blown off the uppermost heights. When ice depth became at least 100 feet – exact thickness depended on degree of slope –, the ice became flexible under great weight and flowed into valleys previously cut by rivers. Eventually the ice masses grew to many hundreds of feet thick.

Plucking and grinding, rivers of ice were giant files and conveyor belts that carved the mountain faces, changed the valley profiles from V's to U's, gouged out basins of future lakes, and dumped the debris from this massive sculpture in ridges of loose rock called moraines. Moraines often dammed streams to form lakes. Other lake basins were scooped from the bedrock as the glacier ground its way downhill.

The last major Ice Age ended 8 to 10 thousand years ago. Probably we live in a warm temperature pulse between advances of ice. An even warmer period some 6,000 years ago melted all traces of the glaciers that sculpted the parks' mountains. Cold periods during the last few thousand years have caused minor glaciers to reform high on the mountains, never flowing down into the valleys that contained their predecessors. But the moving masses of ice are shrinking again. To be still considered a glacier, the ice must move at least a little over the years, and slight movement sometimes is difficult to discern. Most of the snowy accents on the high peaks of Rocky Mountain, Grand Teton, and Glacier/Waterton Lakes are just permanent icefields or perpetual snowbanks. Glaciers are deemed to have melted completely away from Yellowstone.

Wild Animals

Some species of birds and mammals live in one or more of the parks but not in the others. But the following animals live in or near all the parks.

Mammals

Moose are common sightings in Grand Teton, Yellowstone, and Glacier/Waterton Lakes and recently have found their way into Rocky Mountain National Park. Largest member of the deer family, a bull moose may weigh between 900 and 1,400 pounds and boasts huge palmate antlers. Both sexes have long legs, humped shoulders, a bulbous snout, and a flap of skin (the dewlap) hanging from the throat.

Although it looks deceptively ungainly, the moose is superbly adapted to live in the wet environment of mountain lakes, marshes, and stream banks. There it eats aquatic plants, including the leaves and twigs of water-loving shrubs. Moose mate from mid-September to November, and males can be very cranky and dangerous to approach closely during this time. Cows with calves in spring are even less friendly.

Elk are also called by the Indian name wapiti to avoid confusion with the European moose which is known as an »elk.« However, there can be no confusing the regal majesty of this second-largest member of the deer family. The bulls weigh from 600 to 1000 pounds and are excitingly majestic when strutting antlers that may reach 4 to 5 feet in length. Elk both graze on grasses and flowers and browse twigs and bark of deciduous trees and bushes. They are gregarious animals which migrate in herds to lower elevations to escape the deepest snows of winter.

Mule deer are about three feet tall at the shoulders and as lovely as elk are majestic. Their name comes from their big ears, and they also have black-tipped tails. Common and adaptable, mule deer eat a wide variety of grasses, flowers, leaves, and twigs of both evergreens and deciduous trees and shrubs. Mule deer bucks bear branching antlers, which, like moose and elk, they shed in winter.

Bighorn sheep have true horns that are kept permanently by both sexes, rather than the antlers grown each year by male deer. The spike horns of female sheep sometimes cause park visitors to mistake them for mountain goats – often seen in Glacier/Waterton Lakes. Watch for the bighorn's sandy-colored coat and white rump. The massive curled horns of a bighorn ram add a ring each year.

During the early winter mating season, rams duel for dominance and access to ewes by crashing their huge horns together. Sometimes, however, a ritual display of large horns is enough to make a less dominant ram back away.

Bighorns are very gregarious. Ewes and lambs band together separately from the males in summer, but the sexes form mixed bands in winter. These bands feed on high, open meadows in summer, preferably with a rocky area nearby where their broad feet and agility may protect them from predators. In winter, they require wind-blown slopes, where snow is swept away from grass, or the lesser snow depths of lower elevations, where they can paw through to their food.

Coyotes are dog-like predators with a skinny muzzle, long, pointed ears, and a bushy tail. Extremely adaptable, they roam from the plains to alpine meadows. They scavenge winter- and road-killed animals, and prey on animals ranging in size from deer to grasshoppers. But rodents, rabbits, and hares make up the main part of their diet. In fact, coyotes do much to prevent these rapidly reproducing animals from denuding the landscape of edible plants. A coyote chorus of howls, yips, and barks enlivens the wilderness night with a special thrill.

Coyotes might be mistaken for other canine predators. *Gray wolves* are exceedingly rare in Glacier/Waterton Lakes and have been wiped out in the other national parks of the Rockies. But reintroduction may be possible. *Foxes* are much smaller, shy, and rarely seen. The red fox depends largely on a well-developed sense of smell to locate its prey; it also relies on its keen eyesight, speed, and agility to capture mice, hares, birds, and whatever else it can run down or surprise.

Another predator is the *cougar,* or mountain lion, largest of North American cats. It is solitary, mainly nocturnal, and is sometimes seen in Glacier/Waterton Lakes. The cougar, which feeds primarily on deer, requires a large territory. Because of its strength, stealth, and speed, American folklore has given this wary cat a false reputation as a man-stalker. Considerably smaller cats in the national parks are the *lynx* and the *bobcat.*

Bears are seen only by lucky park visitors. In Rocky Mountain, only black bears are found and these very rarely. Both black bears and grizzlies live in the other parks. Both species eat almost anything, and both are unpredictable and dangerous for people to approach closely. Bears are not true hibernators in winter, but do spend most of the season asleep in their dens where they live off fat layers built up in summer. Black bears are the smaller of the two species and have short claws well suited for climbing trees. A hump on a grizzly's shoulders makes it unmistakable. Its long claws are used for digging food – bulbs or burrowing animals –, which makes the claws of mature grizzlies too dull for climbing. Grizzlies can climb sufficiently stout branches like a ladder. Bears usually are solitary, but females remain with their cubs for more than a year and are very protective of them.

In bear country, hikers should strive to avoid confrontations by being noisy. Bear bells worn on packs are popular, but whether or not they work is uncertain. In case of meeting a bear on the trail, a slow retreat by the hiker is in order. Running away may provoke a charge. Bears can outrun even the most intensely motivated human.

The *marten* is a large brown weasel with a buff or yellowish chin and belly. Most at home in forests, this bushy-tailed, lithe hunter also ranges into rocky areas, seeking a wide variety of small animals to eat. Insects and carrion supplement the marten's diet. Although most active at night, martens will hunt by day if hungry and frequently seem unafraid of humans, observing us with as much curiosity as we have for them.

Martens play vigorously among themselves, but the most fun-loving member of the weasel family seems to be the even bigger *river otter.* Largely a matter of luck, a sighting of this aquatic clown is never to be forgotten. It may float on its back, slide on its belly down mud or snow banks into the water, and generally frolic, chattering loudly all the while. An unexcelled swimmer, the river otter feeds mostly on fish.

Wolverines, largest members of the weasel family, are occasionally seen in the subalpine forest of Glacier/Waterton Lakes national parks. They eat almost anything. They have a stout muscular body which is dark brown, and are known for their aggressiveness.

Chipmunks of various species are common throughout all the parks. These sprightly little rodents are distinguished by stripes running the length of their bodies to their noses.

The *golden-mantled ground squirrel* is another striped rodent that is often mistaken for a large chipmunk. However, its stripes do not extend into its face.

Ground squirrels without stripes also live in each park, and they look and act much alike although defined as different species. The *Richardson's ground squirrel* inhabits Rocky Mountain; *Uinta ground squirrel* lives in Grand Teton and Yellowstone; *Columbian ground squirrel* is the species in Glacier/Waterton Lakes. All bear the common name of »picket pin« because they sit upright when they eat grass seeds in open country. This posture reminded early travelers of the stakes that they drove in the ground to tie their horses.

Marmots are woodchuck cousins that inhabit rock piles. The three southernmost parks are home to yellow-bellied marmots. The hoary marmot found in Glacier is both larger and lighter in color. The hoary marmot is also called »whistler« because of its sharp, high-pitched distress call, which is only slightly louder than the very similar call of warning used by yellow-bellies.

The *red squirrel* lives in forests. It eats mushrooms, eggs, and baby birds when available. But the main red squirrel foods are the cambium layers of new-growth twigs and seeds ripped from cones. They cut and store cones for winter food.

The *porcupine* feeds on tree bark. Active mostly at night, this large rodent is seen most often in early morning and late evening. Its barbed quills are an excellent defense against most predators and come loose easily in an attacker's flesh. The porcupine cannot, however, throw its quills.

Beaver dams create many ponds in the parks of the Rocky Mountains. Largest of the park rodents, a beaver may weigh more than 60 pounds and stretch nearly 2 yards long from its nose to the end of its flat tail. Among the most fascinating of North American mammals, the beaver is best known as nature's engineer because it builds dams and lodges of sometimes huge proportions. In summer it eats grass and leaves as well as the bark of the trees it gnaws down for construction materials. In winter, bark of stored branches is its main food.

A *muskrat* cutting a V through the water of a beaver pond is often mistaken for the much larger rodent. When unsure about size, watch for a muskrat's skinny, rat-like tail. Like the beaver, the muskrat may live either in a lodge or in a den dug in the bank of a stream or pond.

The big feet of the *snowshoe hare* are white throughout the year, but the rest of its fur changes from brown to white in winter, except for black tips on the ears. The smallest member of the rabbit clan in the Rockies, the *pika,* is a round-eared dweller of rock piles.

Birds

Five of the most frequently seen birds in the national parks of the Rocky Mountains are members of the jay and crow family. The *Clark's nutcracker* and *gray jay* are both called »camp robber« because they flutter around places where humans congregate, waiting unafraid for the chance to snatch an unguarded bit of food. Often confused with each other, these birds are easy to distinguish because the nutcracker has a long bill with which it extracts seeds from pine cones. The nutcracker also flashes distinctive white and black markings in its wings and tail when it flies.

Two very colorful members of the family are *Steller's jay* and the *black-billed magpie.* The Steller's jay is dark blue with a black head topped by a bobbing crest. With white streaks down its face, the Steller's jay appears to be decked out in war paint and bonnet as its crest flops wildly while the bird pecks vigorously at seeds or other food. The magpie boasts a very long tail that streams unmistakably behind the bird as it flies. Its iridescent green-blue plumage, which sometimes looks black, and flashing white wing patches never fail to impress park visitors.

The black *raven* is the largest member of the crow family. Because its flight pattern is similar to that of the hawk, the raven is often mistaken for it. It also resembles the crow, which is less common than the raven in the Rockies. In addition to its much larger size, the raven has a heavier bill than a crow. And, unlike the fan-shaped crow's tail, the raven's tail is broader in the middle than it is next to the body or at the tip.

Golden and bald eagles are the largest predatory birds in the parks of the Rocky Mountains. The *golden eagle* appears dark when seen soaring high on hot air currents watching for rabbits, marmots, and ground squirrels to eat. Its large size is the best way to distinguish a golden eagle from other soaring predators except immature bald eagles, whose heads do not turn white until the fourth year.

The *bald eagle,* national symbol of the United States, is an endangered species outside of Alaska. Because it feeds primarily on fish and water birds, it is seen mostly around lakes and rivers.

The *osprey* is another fish-eating member of the hawk family. Nicknamed »fish hawk,« an adult osprey needs about one pound of fish each day. It hovers above the water watching for a fish. Spotting its target, the fish hawk dives straight down, often completely submerging, to clasp its prey in specially adapted talons. Then the osprey's strong wings lift bird and a struggling, heavy fish to the surface and then into the air.

A much smaller bird that also seeks its food under the water is the *dipper* or water ouzel. Looking like a large, gray wren, the dipper dives fearlessly into mountain lakes and rushing streams hunting insect larvae or even trout fingerlings. Just when it seems that a turbulent stream has swallowed the dipper permanently, the bird flies out of the water, shakes sparkling water drops from its wings and does a comical, bobbing dance on a wet log or rock. Building its dome-shaped, mossy nest on a rock ledge close to a stream's spray, the dipper never strays from the water. As streams and lakes freeze in winter, dippers follow the streams down to open water.

Plants

The climate of the Rocky Mountains includes a cold winter and a short, warm growing season with generally little moisture. Rocky Mountain soil is usually coarse and infertile. Such growing conditions favor the hardy, needle-leaved conifers. Slopes covered by evergreen forests are typical through most of the range. The few broad-leaved tree species are members of the poplar family and grow best in the wetter environment of water courses.

Six conifer species grow in all of the national parks of the Rocky Mountains. These are lodgepole pine and limber pine, Engelmann spruce, subalpine fir, Douglas-fir, and Rocky Mountain juniper. Quaking aspen and black cottonwood are the only broad-leaved trees found in all the parks, although various species of deciduous shrubs also spread across the slopes of the park areas.

High mountains produce a wide range of microclimates as a function of changes in altitude. Thus, there are many more types of environments that best suit different types of plants than would be found on a flat area of the same

Engelmann Spruce

Blue Spruce

Subalpine Fir

Douglas-Fir

Lodgepole Pine

Limber Pine

Ponderosa Pine

Whitebark Pine

Western Hemlock

Rocky Mountain Juniper

Quaking Aspen

Black Cottonwood

size. This situation permits a very great variety of small plants, particularly showy wildflowers, to grow in the Rocky Mountains. More than 5,000 species of flowering plants cover the whole blooming Rockies.

Being able to put a name on a flower enables the human mind to perceive it separately from another flower. Therefore, the more flowers a person can name, the more variety of flowers that person will see and enjoy. Few, if any, people can name all of the Rocky Mountain wildflowers.

Among the flowers that are the most attention-grabbing in the national parks of the Rocky Mountains are the many species of *Indian paintbrush*. Because paintbrush species hybridize freely, they display an almost infinite variety of colors. Somewhat resembling the shape of an artist's paintbrush, the colorful blossom is actually made up of leaves, while the true flower that produces pollen and seeds is green and inconspicuous.

Columbine species also come in many colors and are easy to identify because of the spurs that jut from the rear of the blossoms. These spurs contain nectar deep inside the blossoms. Therefore, hummingbirds and insects trying to reach the nectar will be forced to brush against the pollen, picking some up on their bodies to carry to fertilize the next flower they visit. However, some insects cut holes in the ends of the spurs to steal the nectar without having to work for it.

Approximately 20 percent of the Rockies' wildflowers are, like dandelions and sunflowers, members of the plant family called *composites*. In composites, many individual flowers group together, simulating one flower head that does the work of many. This is an efficient way to produce seeds while expending the minimum amount of energy needed to attract pollinators. Composites are a relatively recent development in flower evolution, but the system works well and composites are extremely common.

Most composites are approximately disk-shaped, with petals radiating from a center. It at least seems that the bulk of composites are yellow and resemble each other closely, which can make identifying individual species difficult. From this difficulty rises the common name under which many species are lumped, D. Y. C., which means »darned yellow composite.«

Another very common wildflower is *harebell,* which grows from foothills to summits. The Scottish bluebell is a close relative of this flower. Also called witch's thimble, charming harebell evidently gained its name because witches were supposed to be able to turn themselves into hares.

Joe Arnold Jr., Alan Carey, Paul Chesley,
Nicholas DeVore, Halle Flygare, Jeff Foott,
Michael H. Francis, James Frank, Robert C. Gildart,
Fritz Hohermuth, Tom Mangelsen, Tom Pittenger,
Walter H. Saenger, Ron Shade, Dan Tyers

Cover picture: Fritz Hohermuth
Picture on front/end papers: Rick Graetz

A pictorial portrait of the national parks

Rocky Mountain

A conifer stunted by its environment near the summit of Eagle Cliff Mountain overlooks Beaver Meadows. The Mummy Range rises to more than 13,000 feet in the background.

Rocky Mountain

A lake dammed by debris from the Lawn Lake Flood of 1982 reflects Mount Chapin (12,454 feet).

Icicles decorate fallen tree at The Pool, a natural rock basin where a bridge takes hikers and horses across the Big Thompson River.

Rocky Mountain

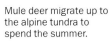 Mule deer migrate up to the alpine tundra to spend the summer.

Clouds occasionally are trapped in Forest Canyon below Trail Ridge Road, while Longs Peak and other mountains stand high above.

The rocky tundra slopes of Trail Ridge provide a good view of Terra Tomah Mountain (12,718 feet).

Rocky Mountain

The mountain bluebird is one of the first migrants to return to Rocky Mountain National Park in spring.

A hairy woodpecker looks for insects to eat on a quaking aspen.

The great horned owl lives in the forests of the Rocky Mountains. Large and powerful, they are capable of taking prey as big as skunks.

Rocky Mountain

Hallett Peak is reflected in Bear Lake as heat of the rising sun generates fog from the lake's surface.

The state flower since 1899, the Colorado blue columbine was given legal protection from picking in 1925.

Snow buttercups decorate the tundra atop Tombstone Ridge.

Rocky Mountain

Within the national park, autumn colors tinge Horseshoe Park below the Mummy Range.

Willow branches in Hidden Valley beaver ponds provide food for the large aquatic rodents. Fairchild

Mountain (13,502 feet) is seen in the background.

Rocky Mountain

Longs Peak is 14,255 feet above sea level, the highest summit in the national park.

Ponderosa pine is the most prominent tree in the montane zone of vegetation.

Rocky Mountain

Cross-country skiing is growing in popularity in Rocky Mountain National Park.

Strong winds and subfreezing temperatures combine to make winter mountaineering and backcountry skiing a frosty encounter.

Skiers on frozen Dream Lake below snow and sun on Hallett Peak (12,713 feet) and Flattop Mountain (12,324 feet).

Rocky Mountain

Fall colors aspen grove on Glacier Knobs as storm clouds threaten above Hallett Peak, left, and Flattop Mountain.

During mating season in early winter, bighorn sheep rams fight each other with curled horns for dominance over a receptive ewe. Butting, shoving, and kicking are common at such times.

Majestic bull elk are common in Rocky Mountain National Park.

Pipe and drum band
marching down Elkhorn
Avenue during Estes
Park's »Scottish High-
land Festival.«

The challenge of bull
riding at the Estes Park
Old Timer's Rodeo is
typical of exciting events
held throughout the
summer at Stanley Field.

Davis Phinney and Ron
Kiefel finish first and
second in Estes Park's
Criterium Race, Coors
Bicycle Classic.

Grand Teton

The jagged peaks of the Teton Range rise almost straight up from the floor of Jackson Hole. At different times and seasons changing light can alter the color of the peaks from rose to lavender to deep grey. Some snow always accents these mountains. The highest peaks are South Teton (12,514 feet), Middle Teton (12,804 feet), Grand Teton (13,770 feet), Mount Owen (12,928 feet), Teewinot Mountain (12,325 feet), as well as Mount Moran (12, 605 feet) further to the north.

Despite their weight of up to 500 pounds, black bears are excellent tree climbers. Their color varies from black to cinnamon; white patches on the chest are not uncommon.

Wildflowers flourish among quaking aspen.

Grand Teton

National park visitors use Jackson Lake for sailing and fishing for cutthroat and other kinds of trout.

The »Cathedral Group« towers above morning mists rising from Jenny Lake.

Grand Teton

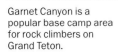
Garnet Canyon is a popular base camp area for rock climbers on Grand Teton.

Rafting on the Snake River is a popular summer activity near Grand Teton National Park.

A kayaker challenges Snake River whitewater.

Grand Teton

Rock climber on Teepe Pillar descends a rope by a technique called rappelling. The granite of the Teton Range offers excellent, stable climbing rock and has made the Tetons one of the top climbing areas in America.

Teton Glacier hangs between the massifs of Grand Teton and Mount Owen.

Grand Teton

The Rocky Mountains compose a symphony of color, blending the summer green of aspen, the reds and yellows of fall, and the brilliant blue of September sky.

Grand Teton

This cattle drive indicates that the century-old livestock industry in Jackson Hole remains important today.

August frost may blanket a meadow in the morning or a saddle left uncovered during the night.

Grand Teton

The natural order of the predator-prey relationship is allowed to take its course in the national parks. Here a coyote feeds on the carcass of a young bighorn sheep which several coyotes had killed; the lamb had suffered from a broken leg and was weakened by deep winter snows.

Pronghorn inhabit Antelope Flats in Jackson Hole. Running at speeds of up to 60 m.p.h. the pronghorn is the fastest North American mammal.

Yellowstone

Morning Glory Pool in the Upper Geyser Basin is named for its resemblance to a morning glory flower. Its temperature ranges seasonally between 158 and 176 degrees F. At the lower temperatures, yellow algae can grow and change a zone of nearby water to green from the normal blue.

The sinter cone of Lone Star Geyser, four miles up the Firehole River from Old Faithful, is 11.5 feet high. It is built by nearly constant splashing of water from the crater, interrupted by 30- to 50-foot eruptions at approximately 3-hour intervals.

Great Fountain Geyser, located near Firehole Lake Drive, is one of Yellowstone's approximately 300 geysers, each of which has its own unique charm. During most eruptions of this geyser one or more bursts will reach about 100 feet. Magnificent bursts reaching 200 feet occur less frequently. Fountain geysers eject their water and steam in several directions from a central pool.

Yellowstone

A short way up Tower Creek from the Yellowstone River, Tower Falls drop 132 feet amid eroded breccia pinnacles for which they are named.

Yellowstone's lakes rank as some of the park's most expressive and serene features.

Yellowstone

Two hikers descend the slopes of Parker Peak (10,203 feet) near the eastern edge of Yellowstone National Park within the Absaroka Range. Open ridges provide seemingly endless views and alpine meadows present colorful displays of wildflowers. Angela Jones studies the trail guide while taking a rest. More than 1,000 miles of trail open the riches of Yellowstone's backcountry to hikers.

Yellowstone

White pelicans watch for fish at the mouth of Pelican Creek on Yellowstone Lake beneath a distant backdrop of the snow-capped peaks of the Absaroka Range, such as Grizzly Peak (9,948 feet), Top Notch Peak (10,238 feet), Mount Doane (10,656 feet), and Mount Stevenson (10,352 feet). Eagle Peak in the Absarokas is the park's highest at 11,358 feet.

Graceful in flight, white pelicans are common near their nesting colonies in Yellowstone Lake between March and August. They fill their large bill pouches with trout from the lake and upper Yellowstone River.

Trumpeter swans, largest of North American swans, once were hunted nearly to extinction, but protection in Yellowstone and nearby Red Rock Lakes National Wildlife Refuge has brought them back from the brink. Trumpeters are often seen in Yellowstone's lakes, ponds, and rivers, here on the Madison River.

Yellowstone

Bison – often inaccurately called buffalo – comprise one of the great success stories of Yellowstone, for here they received protection while being wiped out by hunters elsewhere; only in Yellowstone did wild bison survive.

Yellowstone

Members of the weasel
family, river otters are
excellent swimmers and
capture trout and other
fish as their main source
of nourishment.

The rarely seen bobcat
feeds primarily on
snowshoe hare.

Winter at West Thumb
Geyser Basin presents a
wondrously impressive
conflict between very hot
water and steam and
very cold air.

Yellowstone

In winter snowcoaches, seen here near Norris Geyser Basin, provide public transportation.

Poles installed along the roads during winter help snowmobilers stick to their routes during blizzards.

Dogsleds provide another exciting way to travel Yellowstone roads in winter.

Yellowstone

Water discharged from Mammoth Hot Springs carries limestone dissolved from subterranean chambers and deposits it on the surface in the form of travertine stairs and terraces.

Boiling water in Yellowstone hot springs burns careless visitors each year and has killed some. Therefore, bathing is forbidden in hot water features and their runoff streams. Temperatures become more tolerable where hot water mixes with cold streams such as here at Boiling and Gardner rivers where »hotpotting« is fun in summer and winter.

Bull moose, oblivious to the beauty of fall colors, tend to be irritable and potentially dangerous during this mating season.

Grizzly bears, which often have silver tipped hairs that cause a grizzled appearance, are solitary creatures that usually react with nervous hostility to the approach of another bear.

Yellowstone

The Yellowstone River thunders 308 feet down its Lower Falls into the V-shaped Grand Canyon of the Yellowstone, 20 miles long and as deep as 1,500 feet. Goblinlike hoodoos and steam vents add further drama to the yellow, gold, pink, and brown canyon.

Petrified tree stump on Specimen Ridge.

Yellowstone

The music of flowing water mixes with harmonica strains at the end of a day filled with Yellowstone wilderness.

»Bull Moose« backcountry patrol cabin of the U.S. Forest Service is in Absaroka Beartooth Wilderness, adjacent to the north boundary of Yellowstone National Park. These rustic log cabins were built many decades ago and serve as a ranger's assigned duty station, or simply as an overnight stop on a patrol route.

Pat Hoppe with a packstring on horse patrol in Slough Creek Valley in northeastern Yellowstone, after delivering supplies to a trailcrew in a remote area.

Yellowstone

The Bechler River meanders past lush marshes and oxbow lakes and tumbles down Bechler Canyon while draining plateaus in the southwestern corner of Yellowstone.

Yellowstone provides habitat for the badger, for many other mammals and birds, and for an abundance of wildflowers.

In late May or early June, Yellowstone's cow elk drop their calves; they are born without any scent and with a white-spotted coat that blends in with the dappled sunlight of the forest floor, traits that help them hide from predators.

Lake fishing is one of the most popular wilderness activities; early morning hours provide the best catch.

Rainstorm at sunset pelts Yellowstone Lake with its 110-mile shoreline. The lake is North America's largest at an altitude as high as 7,731 feet.

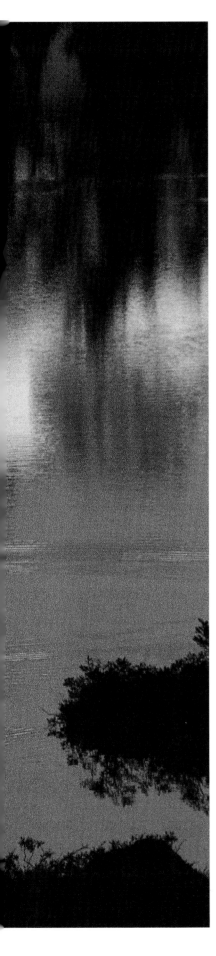

This fire lookout was built atop the wind-whipped summit of Swiftcurrent Mountain (8,436 feet) to exploit a strategic location from which to spot a wisp of smoke in a 100-mile radius and report its location to fire fighters in aircraft.

Sperry Glacier creeps down the steep ridge of the continental divide. The most prominent peaks, from left to right, are: Mount Cannon (8,952 feet), Bearhat Mountain (8,684 feet), and Mount Oberlin (8,180 feet) on the western side – Mount Gould, Reynolds Mountain, Mount Siyeh (10,014 feet), mighty Going-to-the-Sun Mountain (9,642 feet), and the sharp ridge of Fusillade Mountain (8,747 feet) above St. Mary Lake on the eastern side of the continental divide.

A bighorn ram annually adds a growth segment to its massive, curled horns. This ram is approximately six years old, has well-groomed horns and old battle scars on its nose.

Grizzly bears in Glacier National Park rarely weigh more than 500 pounds; their wide roaming means that they might be seen anywhere in the park. Like the smaller black bear, grizzlies are unpredictable and dangerous to approach closely.

Heavens Peak rises to 8,987 feet on the west side of Glacier park.

Wildflowers, such as the red Indian paintbrush, form an impressive display below the west face of the Garden Wall. This high ridge along the continental divide was formed as glacial ice attacked it on both sides, leaving a high, knife-edged wall.

The glacier lily is a lovely companion of melting snowbanks in the subalpine zone to tree line. While Indians used it for food, modern wilderness travelers should only enjoy its enchanting beauty.

Beargrass, large and striking member of the lily family, decorates Glacier's slopes from the park portal at West Glacier to tree line.

Chief Mountain (9,066 feet) is a solitary limestone tower made up of complex layers. Indians revere the mountain and have for years used it in ceremonial acts.

Mountain goats, symbol of Glacier National Park, frequent mineral licks and are often seen as white dots on cliffs above Going-to-the-Sun Road. They eat a wide variety of plants, which enables them to survive year round at elevations above 6,500 feet.

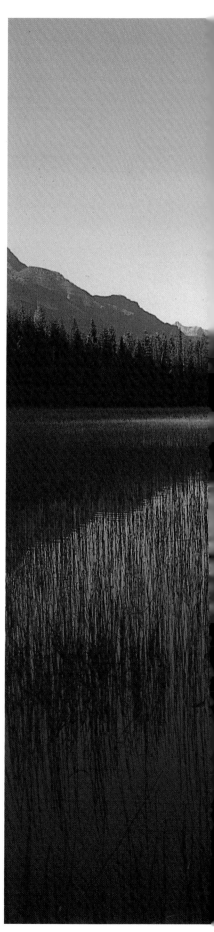

Beaver, largest of the parks' rodents, may weigh more than 60 pounds.

Great blue herons are common around Glacier waters but migrate south for the winter.

The beaver has a reputation as nature's engineer because it builds dams and lodges of sometimes huge proportions, such as this lodge in Baby Bowman Lake below Rainbow Peak.

Thunder and lightning crash in a stormy mountain valley.

The symbol of America, the bald eagle is an endangered species in all states except Alaska. Each fall, bald eagles congregate along McDonald Creek to feed on spawning kokanee salmon.

Ospreys, also called fish hawks, are among Glacier's summer residents, hovering above the park's streams and lakes, such as Upper Kintla Lake, waiting to dive for fish they see below the surface.

The scenery along the trail to Grinnell Glacier is dominated by Mount Gould (9,551 feet) and the Garden Wall, both forming part of the continental divide. The turquoise color of Grinnell Lake is caused by glacial flour carried by meltwaters from Salamander, Gem, and Grinnell glaciers.

The fierce wolverine, a member of the weasel family, is seen occasionally in Glacier and Waterton Lakes national parks. Wolverines prey on small and on larger animals; they also eat any carcass they find as well as some vegetation.

The mountain lion or cougar is a rarely seen resident of the national parks of the Rocky Mountains. It prefers to prey on members of the deer family but also hunts bighorn sheep and goats and small mammals. Because of its strength, stealth, and speed, American folklore has given this wary cat a false reputation as a man-stalker.

Climbers scale a
shoulder of Reynolds
Mountain (9,125 feet), a
giant pyramid astride the
continental divide above
Logan Pass.

Climbing in crevasses, as
seen here in Grinnell
Glacier, is a challenging
activity that should be
undertaken only by those
with proper equipment
and experience.

From Waterton Park townsite, a sightseeing boat cruises south on Waterton Lakes, crossing the U.S.-Canada border into Glacier National Park. Waterton's mountains, as seen here, are Mount Richards (7,850 feet), Bertha Peak (7,613 feet), and Mount Crandell (7,812 feet). Prince of Wales Hotel is an imposing log structure overlooking Waterton Lakes. One of the grand hotels of the Rocky Mountains, it beams welcome to park visitors and provides excellent views of peaks in both national parks, such as West Flattop Mountain (6,830 feet), Porcupine Ridge and Citadel Peaks (7,750 feet), Mount Campbell (8,245 feet), and Mount Richards.

Avalanche Creek, fed by meltwater from Sperry Glacier, has carved its way deeply into red layers of Grinnell argillite. This shady gorge highlights the Trail of the Cedars, accessible from the Going-to-the-Sun Road about 16 miles from the park's West Entrance.

Visiting Rocky Mountain National Park
How To Get There

Many airlines from all over the world serve Denver, a 90-minute drive from the town of Estes Park, eastern gateway to the national park. Bus service links Denver's airport and bus terminal to Estes Park. The town of Grand Lake on the western boundary of the national park is approximately a two-hour drive from Denver. Trail Ridge Road traverses the national park, but the upper stretches are closed by snow in winter.

Accommodations

For information about the wide variety of commercial lodgings and campgrounds along park boundaries, write to the Chamber of Commerce in Estes Park, Colorado 80517, or that of Grand Lake, Colorado 80447. There are five campgrounds within the national park and others nearby in Roosevelt and Arapaho national forests. Some camping spaces in the national park can be reserved. For information about government campgrounds, write to The Superintendent, Rocky Mountain National Park, Estes Park, Colorado 80517, or U.S. Forest Service, 2995 Baseline Road, Boulder, Colorado 80303.

Activities

Things to do in Rocky Mountain National Park include hiking the more than 300 miles of trails, rock climbing, backpacking, fishing, horseback riding, picnicking, cross-country and downhill skiing, observing wildlife, and driving over scenic Trail Ridge, Old Fall River, and Bear Lake roads. Some park roads are plowed in winter.

Special Sights

Spectacular vistas include Longs Peak from Colorado Highway 7 and from Bear Lake and Trail Ridge roads; Hallett Peak from Bear Lake, Forest Canyon Overlook on Trail Ridge Road, Lumpy Ridge from Estes Park and Mac-Gregor Ranch, and Alberta Falls one-quarter mile up Glacier Gorge Trail. Wildflowers are a colorful delight, especially along Cub Lake Trail and in Wild Basin. Watch for the change in zones of plant life while driving up Trail Ridge or Old Fall River roads, paying particular attention to the alpine tundra on Trail Ridge.
Trail Ridge Road also crosses the continental divide at Milner Pass, well below tree line. From this pass, water flows both to the Atlantic and the Pacific oceans. The continental divide zigzags from north to south across the park. Its location is determined by the coincidental shape of the land rather than by altitude. Milner Pass sits at 10,758 feet; Longs Peak is 14,255 feet tall, the highest point in the park, and sits east of the continental divide.

Rocky Mountain National Park

Tundra. The land above the trees. Draped across the tops of peaks towering between 11,000 and 14,255 feet above sea level, the broad expanses of alpine tundra make up the distinctive attraction of Rocky Mountain National Park. In no other national park can visitors experience with such ease so many square miles of this fascinating environment, where an extremely harsh climate permits plants to grow only a few inches above the ground.
The tundra is a world unfamiliar to most travelers who gain access to it on Trail Ridge Road, the highest continuous, paved highway in the United States. This road climbs to 12,183 feet above sea level, and 11 of its 38 + miles snake across the tundra. It is one of the few roads in the Rockies that crosses the mountains by traversing a ridge rather than by climbing a river valley to a pass. Hence, it offers rarely matched opportunities to view spectacular scenery across unobstructed distances.
The narrow band of tree line, the upper limit of tree growth where visitors first encounter the tundra, undulates between 11,000 and 11,500 feet above sea level in the Colorado Rockies. It is the front line in the endless war between woods and wind for control of the mountain tops. Winds that sometimes exceed 200 miles per hour bend, distort, and sandblast pines, spruces, and firs at tree line. Trees that survive portray the staunch character that sometimes comes with abuse and tribulation.
Below the tundra and tree line, two other zones of life – montane and subalpine zones – form irregular bands around the mountains. These are bands of different types of plants established by differences in altitude and exposure to the sun. Motorists driving up Trail Ridge from the park boundary at 8,000 feet travel through the same zones of plants that they would encounter while driving thousands of miles north to the Arctic Circle in Canada or Alaska. To a large extent, the plant zones dictate what kinds of animals can live at particular altitudes on the mountains.
Layering of life zones by differences in altitude was begun by the Laramide Revolution. This buckling of the earth's crust from 65 million to 45 million years ago occurred as North America separated from Europe. Also called the Laramide Orogeny (mountain building), it was the second of three episodes that raised the Rockies. The Colorado Orogeny had raised the Ancestral Rockies some 300 million years ago, but these had been obliterated by erosion when the Laramide Revolution began. From deep within the earth, this mountain-building episode elevated »basement« rocks – formed as long as 1.75 billion years ago – thousands of feet. In jerks and spurts – two feet at one time, 15 feet later, a few inches after that – the mountains rose in slices running north and south through the future Rocky Mountain National Park. Younger, sedimentary rocks that had rested atop

the basement were pushed aside by the uplift, broken, tilted, and eventually washed away.

By 40 million years ago, the mountains uplifted by the Laramide Orogeny were eroded to low, isolated ranges sticking above aprons of their own debris. Within this rolling plain of eroded mountains, rocks decayed under the weathering processes of long ages. Weathering worked its way deep along a grid of cracks created by uplift. Eventually, only isolated cores of unweathered rock remained. Later uplift and washing away of the weathered rock revealed these rounded isolated blocks and boulders on top of Lumpy Ridge, the easternmost arm of Rocky Mountain National Park.

Volcanoes erupted along the western edge of today's national park between 38 and 28 million years ago, creating a few high cones and further burying the uplifted mountains. Much of the park's Never Summer Range resulted from this volcanism. Ashflows from these volcanoes are spectacularly carved by the headwaters of the Colorado River in Little Yellowstone Canyon, enjoyed by hikers along La Poudre Pass Trail.

Yet another uplift between 26 and 10 million years ago caused all of Colorado and parts of adjacent states to rise. The uplift was greatest, about 6,000 feet, along the Colorado Rockies. The rising gave water more erosive power, and it carried away much of the debris that had piled around the mountains of the Laramide Revolution. Peaks 12,000 to 14,000 feet high were uncovered.

Successive advances of glaciers shaped the park's steep-sided peaks and U-shaped valleys as they appear today. One of the best places to visualize the work of the glaciers is in Moraine Park, along the road to Bear Lake. This large meadow is named for the South Lateral Moraine which defines Moraine Park's southern edge. The forest-covered, level-topped ridge which was laid down along the side of a glacier is a perfect, textbook example of a lateral moraine.

Bear Lake itself, at the end of a 9-mile spur road, is dammed by two moraines. From the lake many miles of trails radiate into surrounding glacial valleys, such as Glacier Gorge. Trails from Bear Lake climb also to the tops of ice-carved peaks, including Hallett Peak, which rises dramatically above Bear Lake.

Four small glaciers – Tyndall, Sprague, Andrews, and Taylor – are visited by hikers climbing from the Bear Lake area. These glaciers formed within the last 4,000 years and never left the bowl-shaped basins – cirques – where they originated just below the mountain summits. Three or four terminal moraines in the cirques mark these relatively recent glacial advances: 3,800 to 2,550 years ago, 1,850 to 950 years ago, and during the last 300 years, particularly around 1870. Today, Rocky Mountain National Park's few almost stagnant glaciers barely survive in shady cirques on east- or north-facing slopes.

During the warm periods between glacial advances – the so-called interglacial eras – life moves in to gradually fill the sterile landscape left by the melted ice. The oldest moraines within the cirques have soil on them covered with grassy tundra vegetation. The next oldest support a few pioneer plants on almost no soil. Moraines laid down in the 1870's support only lichens, if any life at all.

During the most recent cold spell of glacial advance, MacGregor Ranch was established in 1874 and still functions within the eastern boundary of the national park. A private educational trust open to the public, MacGregor Ranch preserves a working cattle ranch as part of the area's historic heritage. In the process, it also preserves a lovely, uncluttered setting as foreground to the eroded domes and spires atop dramatic Lumpy Ridge.

In a similar setting on the west side of the national park, Never Summer Ranch demonstrates what life was like on one of Colorado's first dude ranches. The ranch dates back to a 1918 homestead by the German-born Holzwarths, whose Denver saloon had been closed by Prohibition. Seeking a new life in the wilds, husband, wife, son, and two daughters staked out a claim along the headwaters of the Colorado River, adjacent to the newly created Rocky Mountain National Park.

The economic base of the ranch was to have been livestock. But son Johnnie Holzwarth later claimed that all he could raise were »radishes, pansies, and hell.« Moreover, his father's old drinking buddies from Denver kept showing up with only a clean shirt and a bottle of whiskey, looking for a cheap vacation. Johnnie and his mother decided – over the father's protest against charging friends for hospitality – that guests should pay two dollars a day or eleven dollars a week for food, lodging, horses, and a mountain-rimmed setting.

Fifty-four years later, Johnnie Holzwarth sold his guest ranch for preservation within the national park. A complete tour takes about two hours, including trying on backwoods Colorado costumes for fun family photos.

In 1885, Enos Mills arrived on the flanks of Longs Peak, which today is the highest peak in Rocky Mountain National Park, rising to 14,255 feet on the park's east edge. There he began to provide room and board for tourists in 1902. Carving out a career for himself as a conservationist, Mills wrote many articles and books and made many photographs that celebrated the natural wonders of the Colorado Rockies. Beginning in 1909, his message focussed on the theme of creating a national park around the area of Longs Peak. Allied with another local innkeeper, inventor F. O. Stanley, and with the Colorado Mountain Club, Mills gained success in 1915, when Congress established Rocky Mountain National Park.

A unique – for that time – aspect of vacationing at Mills' inn was exposure to a program of nature education on the slopes of Longs Peak. Mills called it a nature school conducted for both children and adults. He pointed out how various plants, animals, and inanimate elements of the mountain environment were all connected with each other. A basic and widely understood concept today, this

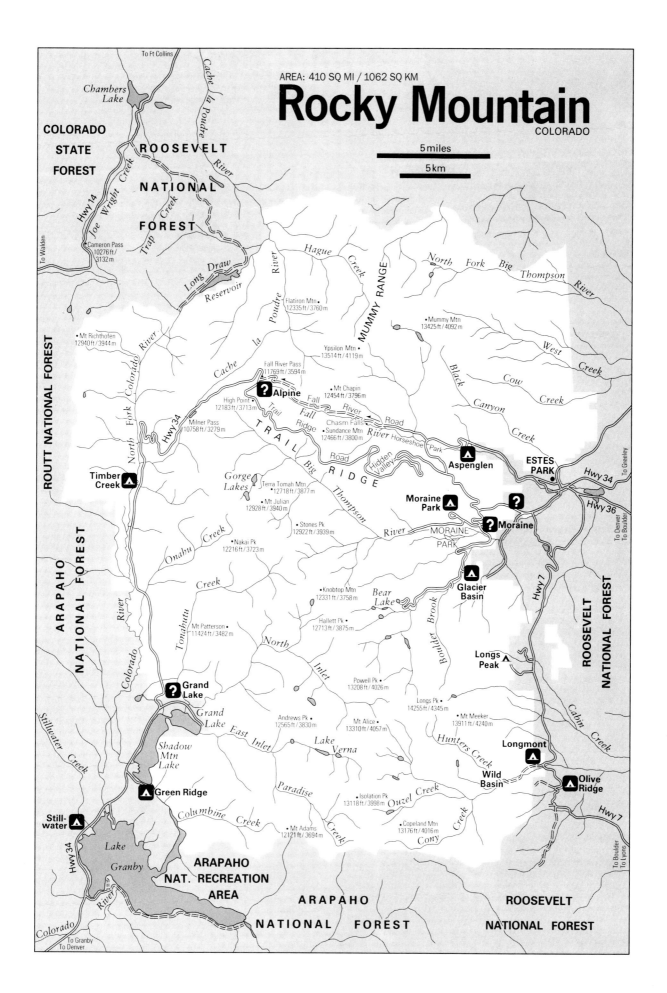

AREA: 410 SQ MI / 1062 SQ KM

Rocky Mountain
COLORADO

5 miles

5 km

To Ft Collins

Chambers Lake

COLORADO STATE FOREST

ROOSEVELT

NATIONAL

FOREST

Hwy 14

Joe Wright Creek

Cache la Poudre River

Cameron Pass 10276 ft / 3132 m

Long Draw Reservoir

Trap Creek

Hague Creek

North Fork Big Thompson River

MUMMY RANGE

Hatiron Mtn • 12335 ft / 3760 m

• Mummy Mtn 13425 ft / 4092 m

West Creek

• Mt Richthofen 12940 ft / 3944 m

Cache la Poudre River

Ypsilon Mtn • 13514 ft / 4119 m

Black Canyon Creek

Cow Creek

ROUTT NATIONAL FOREST

North Fork Colorado River

Fall River Pass 11769 ft / 3594 m

Alpine

• Mt Chapin 12454 ft / 3796 m

High Point 12183 ft / 3713 m

Milner Pass 10758 ft / 3279 m

Fall River

Trail Ridge

Fall River Road

Chasm Falls

• Sundance Mtn 12466 ft / 3800 m

Horseshoe Park

Hidden Valley

ESTES PARK

Hwy 34

To Greeley

Hwy 34

T R A I L   R I D G E

Aspenglen

Hwy 36

Timber Creek

Gorge Lakes

Terra Tomah Mtn • 12718 ft / 3877 m

• Mt Julian 12928 ft / 3940 m

Big Thompson

Road

River

Moraine Park

Moraine

MORAINE PARK

To Denver To Boulder

Onahu Creek

• Stones Pk 12922 ft / 3939 m

• Nakai Pk 12216 ft / 3723 m

ARAPAHO

NATIONAL FOREST

• Knobtop Mtn 12331 ft / 3758 m

Bear Lake

Glacier Basin

Boulder Brook

ROOSEVELT

NATIONAL FOREST

Colorado River

Tonahutu Creek

• Mt Patterson 11424 ft / 3482 m

Hallett Pk • 12713 ft / 3875 m

North Inlet

Longs Peak

Powell Pk • 13208 ft / 4026 m

Hwy 7

Cabin Creek

Grand Lake

Grand Lake

East Inlet

Andrews Pk • 12565 ft / 3830 m

Lake Verna

• Mt Alice 13310 ft / 4057 m

Longs Pk • 14255 ft / 4345 m

• Mt Meeker 13911 ft / 4240 m

Hunters Creek

Longmont

Shadow Mtn Lake

Stillwater Creek

Green Ridge

Paradise

• Isolation Pk 13118 ft / 3998 m

Ouzel Creek

Wild Basin

Olive Ridge

Still-water

Columbine Creek

• Mt Adams 12121 ft / 3694 m

• Copeland Mtn 13176 ft / 4016 m

Cony Creek

Hwy 7

Hwy 34

Lake Granby

ARAPAHO NAT. RECREATION AREA

ARAPAHO

NATIONAL   FOREST

ROOSEVELT

NATIONAL FOREST

Colorado River

To Granby To Denver

To Boulder To Lyons

To Walden

was a new way of approaching nature in the early 1900's. Enos Mills is widely regarded as the founder of the outdoor education techniques utilized by naturalists in national and state parks and nature preserves all over the world.

Mills had the advantage of teaching in an austere environment where the workings of nature are relatively clear and easy to see. The bands of life found while climbing the mountains either by foot or automobile offer good opportunities to compare the effects of different climates on the plants and animals at different altitudes.

Ponderosa pines dominate the montane zone of life, extending from the foothills 30 miles east of the national park to the 9,000-foot elevation, at the lower end of Hidden Valley along Trail Ridge Road. Ponderosas typically grow widely spaced in order that their spreading roots will not compete for available moisture. Especially in wetter-than-usual years, the grassy spaces among ponderosas are carpeted with a multicolored mosaic of wildflowers.

Foresters call this openness »park-like.« The word park has many meanings in Colorado. Of course, Rocky Mountain National Park is an area set aside and managed by the federal government to preserve its natural resources as a kind of open-air museum. It differs radically from the mown lawns and pruned trees of city parks, such as Bond Park within the village of Estes Park on the edge of Rocky Mountain National Park.

The town got its name from the open, peak-surrounded valley in which it sits, a valley settled in 1859 by Joel Estes. Such valleys are usually called parks in Colorado. Similar parks are Moraine and Horseshoe parks within Rocky Mountain National Park, which is called »the Park« by residents of Estes Park.

Parks have always been favored places for human settlement in the Colorado Rockies. They are relatively level, close to water, open to views and sunshine, yet with forests nearby. Before Rocky Mountain National Park was established, many ranches and homes were built in parks within today's national park. The community in Moraine Park was even significant enough to have its own post office. Most of these inholdings have been purchased and their buildings removed by the National Park Service. Buildings not removed sometimes have been preserved for their historic value and used for park administrative purposes.

Not all of the montane zone is ponderosa pine parks. Shady Douglas-fir forests grow thickly on north-facing slopes, where the sun shines less directly and water evaporates less quickly. Douglas-fir also dominates the montane zone on the west side of the national park, which receives more precipitation. Needing even more moisture than the Douglas-fir, the blue spruce decorates the edges of streams and lakes within the montane zone. This conical beauty is the state tree of Colorado and is widely cultivated as an ornamental planting around buildings.

The montane zone is favored as home not only by humans, but by many types of wild animals as well. Most of the large mammals – deer, elk, and bighorn sheep – historically migrated into the montane zone to escape the harsh winter conditions of higher elevations. This natural pattern was disrupted by human settlement, but efforts to give vital montane habitat back to the wildlife have been successful. The park's winter range, however, is very limited. Many animals need to migrate outside park boundaries where techniques must be developed to reduce the competition between humans and wildlife for living space.

Abert's squirrels reside in ponderosa forests throughout the year. Nearly house-cat sized, with tufted ears of rabbit proportions and a flowing tail, Abert's are the showiest of North American squirrels. They can be all black, gray above and white below, or a dark, rusty brown. Totally dependent on ponderosa pines, Abert's squirrels rarely venture far from these trees. They eat ponderosa seeds, when they are available. In winter, their favorite food is the cambium layer of new growth twigs on young ponderosas. Stately, 300-year-old pines provide Abert's nest sites.

The montane zone is also home to many birds. Evening grosbeaks and pygmy nuthatches live there all year. Mountain bluebirds and broad-tailed hummingbirds are among the first migrants to arrive in spring and the last to leave in fall. Golden eagles soar above the summits, but plummet into the montane zone to catch unwary Richardson's and golden-mantled ground squirrels.

Lodgepole pines and quaking aspens usually are the first trees to move into an area swept clear of ponderosas and Douglas-fir by forest fire. These pioneer trees also extend their range above the montane into the subalpine zone, between 9,000 and 11,000 feet above sea level. Lodgepoles usually appear on drier soil, frequently in such dense stands that little vegetation can grow on the forest floor. Hence, lodgepole forests offer less food for most animals than do other areas of the park. In such »doghair« stands, it is unusual to see a large lodgepole. Most of the trees are skinny and were used by Indians who came up from the plains to cut tipi poles for their skin lodges.

Fires sweep easily through doghair lodgepole stands, killing most of the trees. Lodgepole bark is very thin, unlike the thick bark of mature ponderosas, which armors them from all but the fiercest of fires. Through death, however, lodgepoles continue life. Their cones open only in the presence of heat, often remaining tightly closed on the branches for years. When heat from a fire opens the cones, a seed storm rains down on the newly cleared ground. A new lodgepole stand is begun before the ruin cools.

The most recent large fire in Rocky Mountain National Park was started by lightning in 1978 in Wild Basin, the southeastern part of the park. Hikers along Wild Basin trails now enjoy wildflowers, such as fireweed, that are the flags of life advancing into the desolated land. Lodgepole seedlings foretell the forest of the future. Without periodic fires, most of the park's lodgepole forests would eventually disappear. The natural forest of undisturbed subalpine regions is composed of Engelmann spruce and subalpine fir. These shade-loving species grow densely in well-watered sites. But the sun bakes away vital water in open burned areas. When sun-loving lodgepoles grow up, they provide shade in which spruce and fir seeds can germinate. Over the centuries, short-needled spruces and firs grow taller than the lodgepoles and shade them out.

Spruces and firs can also choke out quaking aspens that often grow in moist areas after a forest has been cleared by fire or avalanche. This member of the poplar family does not feed fires to preserve itself. Instead it feeds beavers.

These largest of the park's rodents prefer soft aspen trunks for cutting to build dams and lodges. The soft, white bark is good beaver food. Beavers travel far over land to cut aspens and build canals to float trees to ponds. Finally, however, they may eat themselves out of house and home, eliminating their main food supply within reasonable transportation distance.

But aspens grow very well from their roots. Many trunks within a stand are connected beneath the ground. After the trunk is cut, a new one begins to sprout from the stump or from adjacent roots. Unless beavers can get by on smaller shrubs, they will desert an area after they have depleted the aspens. This gives the trees a chance to redevelop from the old roots. In the event of a devastating forest fire, protected roots quickly send up a new forest of sun-loving aspens.

After beavers desert an area, their ponds silt in, gradually drying out to marshes, then meadows. As the ground dries, aspen pioneers fill the meadows. If beavers return, these aspens are the first to go.

Loss of aspen-eating beavers allows aspen groves to grow taller, providing cool shade for young spruces and firs. These evergreens eventually crowd out the aspens by cutting them off from light. The return of fire or beaver ponds destroy the evergreens and restart the cycle.

Quaking aspen leaves have chlorophyll on both sides. The leaf blades are set at right angle to their petioles (stems), a very unstable attachment. The leaves quake in the slightest breeze, exposing chlorophyll on both sides to sunshine, which powers the food-making activity in the leaves.

Aspen leaves are most obvious in autumn, when they turn many shades of yellow and orange. Within the national park, aspen fall color lines waterways in Beaver Meadows, Moraine Park, and Horseshoe Park. The most spectacular aspen display is the subalpine Bear Lake area, where hundreds of acres were cleared by a forest fire in 1900.

Subalpine trails through spruce-fir forests are some of the most pleasant in Rocky Mountain National Park. Shaded and cool, they traverse the wettest life zone. Here snow blown from the summits accumulates in piles that do not melt completely until July. Spruce-fir forests are natural reservoirs, slowly releasing water from their shaded snowbanks to keep clear mountain streams flowing throughout the year. Their value in this arid land is incalculable. They are the fountains of water, the fountains of life, for most of the Rocky Mountain region.

Deer, elk, and bighorn sheep summer in the subalpine zone, but the dominant creatures, at least in their own estimation, are the diminutive red squirrels. Their chattering alarm calls are very familiar to hikers on park trails, claimed by squirrels as personal fiefs.

These abundant little squirrels are ventriloquists and are sometimes easier to hear than to see. But many piles of cone scales indicate where squirrels have ripped apart cones to get their seeds. Denuded cone cores are tossed among the scales. Scale piles many feet thick covering several square yards – »squirrel kitchens« – are sometimes used to store unopened cones. The cool damp interior of the cone scale midden keeps the cones from opening, sealing the seeds inside, safe from spoiling. Because lodgepole cones do not open anyway, the squirrels often merely leave them on top of the midden.

Much larger and quieter residents of the subalpine zone are the snowshoe hares. They have very large hind feet that give support on deep and long-lasting subalpine snows. Whether in rusty-brown summer garb or in the white of winter, snowshoe hares are hard to spot. But their tracks in the snow are everywhere obvious to cross-country skiers who weave through the park's best life zone for winter recreation.

Limber pines grow in sandy, rocky soil in all the park's life zones but are most distinctive at tree line, where they earn their name. Their very pliable branches bend before the constant wind and thereby survive without breaking. In the process, they grow in fantastic, distorted shapes. The wind distorts spruces and firs at tree line by simply killing any part of them that dares to stand upright against its power. The forest creeps upslope one seed at a time with almost geological slowness.

A tree may very gradually expand beyond protecting rocks by growing new shoots in the lee of its own dead wood. It may even join with other trees expanding from other sheltered spots to form impenetrable wind-pruned hedges at tree line. These distorted leaders of the forest's advance are called »krummholz,« a German term for crooked trees. Another form of krummholz is the banner tree, where the trunk provides protection for branches to live on one side, while wind kills all new growth shoots on the unprotected sides.

Above tree line is the tundra, the arctic-alpine zone which is very similar to the vast treeless regions of Alaska, Canada, and Siberia. One-third of Rocky Mountain National

Park is alpine tundra. During the summer, it is easy to reach by highway and by hiking trail. The national park's tundra is the crowning glory and climax of a passage through the life zones.

Tundra plants hug the ground to be able to survive – just barely – in an environment extremely hostile to life. Besides hiding below the worst of the wind's blasts, many tundra plants are fuzzy to reduce water loss in the desiccating wind. Their fuzz also preserves warmth in a setting where snow can fall any day of the year.

The tundra is not always a grim and austere place, however. In its brief blooming period, the tundra floral display is an explosion of color in the foreground of unobscured vistas of craggy, snow-accented peaks. Most flowers burst open around the end of June and beginning of July.

All but one of the flowers are perennials, for plants usually need more than one short growing season to reproduce themselves on the tundra. Most flowers expend much energy producing blossoms relatively large for such small plants. This high advertising budget is necessary to attract as many insects as possible to pollinate and fertilize seeds that must be spread before the short summer ends here in August.

The largest blossoms belong to alpine sunflowers, two to four inches across and always facing east. The sunflowers spend years storing energy in fleshy tap roots. When preparations are complete, the blooms burst forth. Then, the show over, the pollinators attracted, the seeds set, the plants die.

Various animals feed on these tundra plants. The little, round-eared rabbit relative called a pika actually harvests, dries, and stores these plants like hay for its winter food supply. Looking exactly like the rocks among which it lives, the pika is difficult to see. But its high-pitched, short squeak or bark is a common sound to tundra travelers. Pikas are abundant at Rock Cut, a turnout along Trail Ridge Road, where a tundra nature trail begins.

Mule deer and elk summer on the tundra. And a few especially hardy elk even subject themselves to the frigid misery of winter in the alpine zone.

Bighorn sheep seem particularly suited to scrambling about on rocks above tree line. Most bighorn in the national park also winter on the tundra, where wind sweeps away snow to reveal plants to eat. But biologists feel that staying above tree line all year is unnatural bighorn behavior, caused by past human interference with winter migration to a lower altitude. Although bighorn seem very conservative about moving to new territory, the National Park Service has had some success with inducing sheep to come down from the heights in bitter weather. Hopefully, this will reduce stress on the bighorn population within the national park and allow it to increase.

Predictably, few bird species nest on the treeless tundra. But alpine grouse, called white-tailed ptarmigan, thrive above the trees, in part because they are unsurpassed camouflage artists. In summer, they look exactly like lichen-dotted tundra rocks. Their pure white winter feathers blend with snow drifts piled in krummholz and willow thickets at tree line. Here ptarmigan feed on willow buds and take shelter from fierce winds by burying themselves in the snow.

Nesting in holes in alpine cliffs with snowbanks nearby, rosy finches are common on the tundra in Rocky Mountain National Park. Although their pink and buff feathers are pretty, these birds are not particularly conspicuous while searching for dead insects and seeds imbedded in the snow. Bird watchers, though, flock to see rosy finches at Lava Cliffs at 12,000 feet along Trail Ridge Road. Easy to find there, rosy finches are rarely seen below tree line.

Many creatures are easy to see in Rocky Mountain National Park where life zones are stacked conveniently atop each other within a short distance on the mountain slopes. Vegetation blankets the mountains, but an arid climate keeps it from being lush and hiding the animals. The stresses that life must undergo and the battles it must wage to survive in these rugged mountains are interesting, inspiring, and simple to observe. That the hard-won victory of life takes place amid such awesome grandeur insures us that, whether or not the mountain uplift has stopped, the uplift of the human spirit continues in Rocky Mountain National Park.

Visiting Grand Teton National Park
How To Get There

In the northwest corner of Wyoming, Grand Teton National Park is 500 miles on good highways from Denver, Colorado, and 270 miles from Salt Lake City, Utah. The town of Jackson, the park's southern gateway, also has commercial air and bus service. Grand Teton is less than 7 miles south of Yellowstone National Park, and the two are linked by the John D. Rockefeller, Jr., Memorial Parkway, also administered by the National Park Service.

Accommodations

For information about the many motels, lodges, and commercial campgrounds near the park boundaries, write to the Jackson Hole Chamber of Commerce, Jackson, Wyoming 83001. A wide variety of lodging and six National Park Service campgrounds are also available within the park; for information about them contact The Superintendent, Grand Teton National Park, Moose, Wyoming 83012.

Activities

Things to do in Grand Teton National Park include hiking the more than 200-mile trail system, rock climbing, backpacking, fishing, horseback riding, picnicking, boating, rafting on the Snake River, observing wildlife, visiting the Indian Arts Museum at Colter Bay, the Chapel of the Transfiguration, and various historic sites, and driving the 167 scenic miles of paved road. Downhill skiing is available just outside the park boundaries at Jackson and Teton Village. A 2.4-mile aerial tram at Teton Village lifts its passengers to the 10,450-foot crest of Rendezvous Mountain for a unique perspective on the Teton Range and Jackson Hole. A 12.3-mile trail from the top of Rendezvous enters the national park and is mostly downhill into Granite Canyon and back to Teton Village.

Special Sights

Popular roadside vistas include the so-called Cathedral Group from String Lake, Jenny Lake, Jackson Lake, Oxbow Bend, Hidden Falls and Inspiration Point, and the Teton Range from Signal Mountain. Trails lead to such magnificent sights as Grand Teton from Lake Solitude and the three Tetons from Hurricane Pass.

Grand Teton National Park

There are many peaks in the Rockies that are higher than the Tetons. But none are more dramatic. Rising 7,000 feet directly from their base, without the moderating influence of lower foothills, the Tetons cut a jagged profile across the Wyoming sky. They are ideal mountains, what any small child's drawing of mountains looks like.

The Tetons are the stuff of fairy tale illustrations. It would seem that no mountains really could look like that. Yet these peaks have the hard reality of granite and metamorphic rock. Perhaps it is this solid intrusion of myth and fantasy into the real world that makes visitors gasp a bit the first time they behold the Tetons, or the second time. Indeed, these peaks are breathtaking any time they are viewed with eyes unglazed by the complacency that sometimes accompanies daily association with greatness.

The Shoshone Indians who roamed this area – and still live not far away – called the peaks »Tee-win-ot,« as modern people now call one of the most prominent summits in the range. The name meant, logically enough, »many pinnacles,« and the Shoshones believed these mountains were the dwelling place of holy spirits. Spiritually inclined people today assume the Shoshone were correct, for photographs of the Tetons frequently grace a wide range of religious publications. The tiny Chapel of the Transfiguration, a log Episcopal church within Grand Teton National Park, is probably the most famous house of worship in the United States. Its backdrop of mountain glory far surpasses the noblest efforts of the world's most talented human architects who devoted their lives to the building of cathedrals.

Yet, not all people have understood the grandeur of this special place. In 1818, a group of Iroquois Indians had been trappers in the European fur trade for so many generations that they even had French names and used the French language. These Iroquois were stationed in today's Idaho by the North West Company, based in Montreal. Not inspired by the profit motive of their employers, the Indian trappers soon became tired of chasing beaver and headed east. On their way, they viewed three snowy peaks to the east, across a valley now named for one of the Iroquois, Pierre's Hole. The lusty trappers called the peaks »Les Trois Tetons« – The Three Breasts.

Although the name stuck to South Teton, Middle Teton, and Grand Teton – at 13,770 feet, the tallest peak in the range –, the mountains' natural sublimity has overwhelmed history's vulgarity. Today, when Americans hear of the Tetons, the immediate image brought to mind is a picture of the Western Hemisphere's most famous mountain vista – the Teton Range from Jackson Hole. In the vicinity of Grand Teton National Park, residents refer to the park's namesake with reverence as simply »The Grand.«

»Hole« is another term that has a unique local meaning. Fur trappers called an open valley surrounded by mountains a hole. Jackson Hole, named for fur trapper David Jackson, is such a valley, 8 miles wide and 50 miles long on the east side of the Teton Range. The largest town within Jackson Hole is simply called Jackson.

Jackson Hole actually is a hole of sorts. It is a block of the earth's crust that has dropped along a fault, a crack in the crust at the base of the Tetons. The peaks themselves are the east edge of another block that rose along the same crack, called the Teton fault zone.

The mountains tilted up as though hinged on the Idaho-Wyoming border, and the valley tilted down as though hinged on the east. Total movement of originally connected rocks within the two blocks up and down from each other has been about 30,000 feet. Erosion, however, tore down the mountains as they rose and filled the valley, reducing the difference in altitude to 7,000 feet. The shifting of valley and peak tops away from each other began about 10 million years ago, making the Tetons very young relative to the age of most of the Rockies of approximately 60 million years. Movement along the fault has averaged 4 inches per century and still continues today.

The Tetons are an asymmetrical range, highest on the precipitous east edge of the fault block. They slope more gradually to the west toward their »hinge« with the earth's crust. The steepness on the east gives water, ice, and gravity more power to erode and carve the mountains into their dramatic forms.

Carving by mountain glaciers gave the Tetons their present craggy beauty. The classic forms of Teton glaciation are well presented from the top of Signal Mountain, a low peak rising from the middle of Jackson Hole and ascended by a five-mile spur from Teton Park Road. On the face of Mount Moran, nearest of the high peaks to this point, Skillet Glacier hangs with its »handle« nearly at the top of Moran. The dozen modern Teton glaciers are not remnants of the Ice Age peak-carvers. Rather, they date from more recent cold spells, perhaps the Little Ice Age of the 13th Century A.D. Most mountain glaciers originated in bowl-shaped cirques that all along the range mark where the ice rivers plucked and carved the rock at their headwalls.

Directly below Mount Moran, Jackson Lake sits in a glacier-formed basin. But it was artificially enlarged by a man-made dam in 1916 to store more water for irrigation. The islands in the lake are tops of moraines dumped by the melting ice sheet.

Along the line of peaks, canyons clearly display the U-shape caused by glaciers widening the floors and steepening the walls of originally V-shaped canyons carved by stream erosion. At the foot of each canyon is the tree-covered terminal moraine deposited where the most recent glacial advance stopped. Below the trinity of pointed peaks called the Cathedral Group – Teewinot Mountain, Grand Teton, and Mount Owen –, the edge of Jenny Lake is barely visible behind one of these natural moraine dams. Hidden west of their moraines are other lakes – Leigh, Taggart, Bradley, and Phelps – all created by glaciers flowing out of Teton canyons about 10,000 to 12,000 years ago. Moraines formed by glaciers some

50,000 years earlier dammed Two Ocean and Emma Matilda lakes, northeast of Signal Mountain.

From the top of Signal Mountain, older moraines appear as long, forested ridges crossing the floor of Jackson Hole. As a legacy of older, more extensive glaciation, the moraines contain clay formed from rocks ground to powder inside the rivers of ice. This clay holds moisture that supports tree growth. The sands and gravel of glacial outwash on the flat lands beyond the moraines allow water to drain away and can support only dryness-tolerant plants associated with sagebrush.

Small lakes glistening from the floor of Jackson Hole in an area called The Potholes mark former sites of isolated blocks of ice within glacial outwash debris. Insulated by the surrounding rock and dirt, the ice melted very slowly. When the ice blocks finally did disappear, depressions were left that collect water. Bison are often seen in The Potholes area.

Although the scenery of the Tetons towering over Jackson Hole is relatively young, the rocks in the mountains were formed more than 2 billion years ago. Originally laid down as sediments or volcanic deposits on the floor of an ancient sea, these layers were buried, squeezed, heated, folded, and crushed under miles of overlying rock until the identities of the original rocks were obliterated. What remained were the squiggly patterned gneiss and crystalline schist that form Mount Moran.

A half billion years later, molten rock squeezed its way through the metamorphic schist and gneiss, eventually cooling to granite, laced with light lines of pegmatite. These igneous rocks are particularly evident in the central part of the range, in the Cathedral Group and Mount Moran. Hot rock flowed again about 1.3 billion years ago, penetrating the granite, schist, and gneiss to form dark bands of diabase. A vertical diabase dike is prominent below the summit on the east face of Mount Moran.

During the long ages that followed, miles of sedimentary rocks accumulated atop the metamorphic and igneous rocks of today's Tetons. A scant remnant of the sedimentary rocks forms a light-colored cap atop Mount Moran. More are found in the western, southern, and northern extremes of the range. But the vast bulk of these layers was eroded away, particularly during the Laramide Orogeny 60 to 70 million years ago when most of the Rocky Mountain ranges were uplifted. The Teton area rose with the rest, and the rise gave extra power to forces of erosion. Erosion debris filled basins between mountains, and, together with volcanic ash blown in from Yellowstone, leveled the terrain of today's Grand Teton National Park.

At last, some 8 to 10 million years ago, the Teton block and Jackson Hole began to tilt away from each other along the Teton fault zone. Most overlying sedimentary rock was washed away as steepening terrain again empowered erosion. The scenic core of Teton rocks emerged to await the sculpturing that would refine them

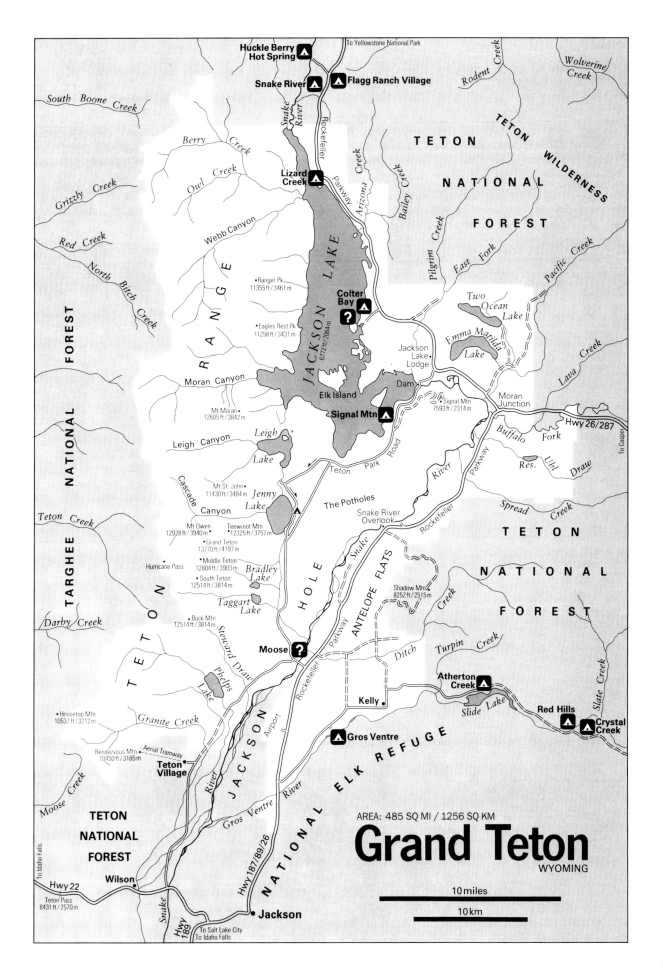

Huckle Berry
Hot Spring

To Yellowstone National Park

Snake River   Flagg Ranch Village

Rodent   Creek

Wolverine
Creek

South Boone Creek

Berry   Creek

Owl   Creek

Lizard
Creek

Snake River

Rockefeller Parkway

Arizona Creek

Bailey Creek

Pilgrim Creek

TETON

WILDERNESS

Grizzly Creek

Red Creek

North Bitch Creek

Webb Canyon

JACKSON   LAKE
6772ft/2064m

•Ranger Pk
11355ft/3461m

Colter
Bay

•Eagles Rest Pk
11258ft/3431m

East Fork

NATIONAL

Two
Ocean
Lake

FOREST

Pacific Creek

Emma Matilda
Lake

RANGE

Moran Canyon

Jackson
Lake
Lodge

Elk Island

Lava Creek

Dam

Mt Moran•
12605ft/3842m

Signal Mtn

•Signal Mtn
7593ft/2314m

Moran
Junction

Leigh Canyon

Leigh
Lake

Teton   Park   Road

Buffalo   Fork

Hwy 26/287

To Casper

Cascade

Mt St. John•
11430ft/3484m

Jenny
Lake

Canyon

The Potholes

Snake River
Overlook

Res.

Uhl   Draw

Teton Creek

Mt Owen•
12928ft/3940m

Teewinot Mtn
•12325ft/3757m

•Grand Teton
13770ft/4197m

Snake

Rockefeller

Spread   Creek

TETON

TARGHEE

•Middle Teton
12804ft/3903m

Bradley
Lake

HOLE

Parkway

NATIONAL

Hurricane Pass

•South Teton
12514ft/3814m

Darby Creek

•Buck Mtn
12514ft/3814m

Taggart
Lake

River

Shadow Mtn
8252ft/2515m

NATIONAL

FOREST

TETON

Steward Draw

Antelope Flats

Creek

FOREST

Moose

Phelps
Lake

Turpin   Creek

•Housetop Mtn
10537ft/3212m

Granite Creek

JACKSON

Rockefeller   Parkway

Ditch

Atherton
Creek

Slide Lake

Slate Creek

Red Hills

Crystal
Creek

Kelly

Airport

Gros Ventre

Rendezvous Mtn
10450ft/3185m

Aerial Tramway

Teton
Village

Snake   River

Gros Ventre   River

NATIONAL   ELK   REFUGE

AREA: 485 SQ MI / 1256 SQ KM

Grand Teton
WYOMING

Moose Creek

TETON

NATIONAL

FOREST

To Idaho Falls

Hwy 22

Wilson

Teton Pass
8431ft/2570m

Snake

Hwy 189

Hwy 187/89/26

Jackson

To Salt Lake City
To Idaho Falls

10 miles

10 km

to the essence of mountain beauty.

The erosion which stripped the Teton core of its sedimentary mantle became less abstract on June 23, 1925. Suddenly 50 million cubic yards of dirt and rock broke loose from Sheep Mountain a few miles east of the national park. In three minutes, the mass roared 2,000 feet down into the valley at 50 miles per hour and continued on about 400 feet up the opposite ridge. The rubble dammed the Gros Ventre River, forming Slide Lake. Marking the former location of the rubble is a bare gash more than 1.5 miles long, 0.5 mile wide, and as deep as several hundred feet on the hillside above the lake. Almost two years later, after a heavy spring runoff of melting snow, water flowed over the top of the new dam, dislodging the top 50 feet of rock at the south end. Water rushed out of Slide Lake in a flash flood that wiped out the little town of Kelly.

Eventually, all lakes either break their dams or fill with sediment. The hiking trail up the South Fork of Cascade Canyon, for instance, climbs up a stairstep terrain formed by the filling of ponds. Some ponds were created by glacial excavation from bedrock, others by small moraines deposited by the retreating glacier, still others by beavers. These pond sediments nourish large whitebark pine, Engelmann spruce and subalpine fir, and abundant wildflowers.

The giant step up into the canyon from the level of Jenny Lake, however, was created differently. The first of three mountain glaciers that shaped the canyon during the last 150,000 years could not excavate Teton granite as fast as a much larger glacier flowing past from Yellowstone could cut into the soft sediments on the floor of Jackson Hole. The Yellowstone glacier's faster cutting left the mouth of Cascade Canyon and its glacier hanging some 250 feet above Jackson Hole. Today Hidden Falls cascades over the rim formed by the passage of the larger glacier.

It seems too obvious to mention that the more than 200 miles of hiking trails in Grand Teton National Park offer joy beyond measure and literally limitless delights to the eye. Most hikers follow the shores of lovely morainal lakes at the canyon mouths or follow the canyons among the mountains. A favorite destination is Lake Solitude, which offers a fine view of Grand Teton but little solitude during good hiking weather in summer. Part of the trail's popularity derives from its continuation over the high country of Paintbrush Divide. From there a descent into Indian Paintbrush Canyon leads down to String Lake in a two-day circle trip.

Who can gaze at the Tetons and not wonder what it would be like to stand on their summits? Climbers flock to these young mountains. The National Park Service requires hikers who camp overnight or climb in the Teton backcountry to obtain permits. The permitting procedure provides an opportunity to warn climbers about rock falls and dangerous ice and snow. But the dangers can be avoided with care, and it is a rare day in midsummer when a dozen climbers do not reach the top of The Grand.

John D. Rockefeller, Jr., Memorial Parkway was established in 1972 in recognition of the man who had bought a total of 32,189 acres in Jackson Hole and donated them to the park in 1950. This philanthropy resulted in the enlargement of the park from its original boundaries, which included only the east slope of the high peaks and the lakes at their base, excluding Jackson Lake. Rockefeller's action preserved the foreground that is vital to this magnificent scene.

The parkway, which extends from Grand Teton's south boundary up to Grant Village in Yellowstone National Park, traverses sagebrush flats in Grand Teton. At turnouts along the road, National Park Service exhibits explain geology, plant life, wildlife, history, and other facts of interest. The Snake River Overlook is deservedly popular because the curves of the park's main watercourse direct the eye pleasantly up to the magnificent spire of Grand Teton.

The Rockefeller Parkway is the fastest route through the national park and the only one open in winter. It is not, however, the most scenic route, a statement difficult to believe while watching the incredible scenery go by.

In a national park where all roads offer superlative vistas, the Teton Park Road along the base of the range manages to be better than best. A visitor center at the road's southern end near Moose Entrance Station provides visitor information and orientation. Nearby is the Chapel of the Transfiguration, built in 1925.

Beyond the chapel, Teton Park Road follows the course of Cottonwood Creek. Constantly changing views of mountains towering above cause many motorists to miss seeing moose along the creek. Wildflowers, such as arrowleaf balsamroot, make a colorful foreground for the austere peaks. About two miles from the entrance station is the popular trailhead for Taggart and Bradley lakes.

In the vicinity of Jenny Lake, the skyline recomposes itself into the imposing cluster of the Cathedral Group. The Jenny Lake Road is a one-way loop from its north junction with the Teton Park Road. From the Jenny Lake Road, the Cathedral Group is seen in its most glorious configuration, especially awesome when reflected in String Lake.

From String Lake, the Jenny Lake Road traverses the forested moraine that dams Jenny Lake. From an overlook, it is easy to imagine the ice flowing from U-shaped Cascade Canyon and occupying the space now filled by water.

The end of Teton Park Road is at Jackson Lake Junction. Down in Willow Flat, between the road and Jackson Lake, is a good place to look for moose; another good place is along the road between Jackson Lake Junction and Buffalo Entrance Station. At Oxbow Bend, a meander now abandoned by the main channel of the Snake River, visitors may see not only moose, but muskrat, beaver, river otter, trumpeter swan, white pelican, sandhill crane, osprey, Canada goose, bald eagle, and a variety of ducks. All this wildlife frequently disturbs a perfect reflection of Mount Moran.

Abundant wildlife has lured humans to Jackson Hole perhaps since ancient hunters searched for game in the chill shadows of glaciers flowing from Teton canyons. Certainly various Plains Indian tribes in historic times made warm-weather visits to hunt elk, pronghorn, and bison. The bitter cold winters of Jackson Hole discouraged year-round Indian habitation.

It was beaver that brought white fur traders and trappers – the mountain men – to Jackson Hole between 1807 and 1840. In one of America's most spectacular settings were acted out in those decades some of America's most spectacular adventures. Indian battles, lonely murders, killing cold, and brutal trade wars between rival fur companies highlighted a history made in the shadow of the Tetons.

Economics and over-trapping eventually made the trade in beaver pelts unprofitable. In the 1870's, Federal surveys and the frontier artistry of photographer William H. Jackson and painter Thomas Moran revealed the Tetons to the world. Wealthy adventurers were attracted to the wildlife and scenery. But not until the 1880's did permanent settlers attempt to establish a livestock-raising economy in Jackson Hole.

Probably the area was no more lawless than many other frontier communities during this time. But its dramatic setting, seeming to exaggerate the wonders of nature, perhaps inspired writers of fiction to exaggerate the unusual events of human lives in Jackson Hole. In any case, novelist Owen Wister visited the area in 1887 and was inspired to write *The Virginian*. This novel set in Jackson Hole established the classic figure of the cowboy in the »Wild West« as a fixture in American literature.

Modern ranches along the Antelope Flats Road still convey a sense of the old West with a backdrop of the Teton Range. The Joe Pfeifer Homestead, purchased by the National Park Service in the mid-1960's, also preserves the mood of early Jackson Hole ranching in its tumbledown log buildings.

As Jackson Hole filled with ranches, domestic livestock began to crowd out the elk herds that for centuries had migrated into the valley in winter to feed on its broad pastures. Early settlers depended on elk for food, and commercial hunters made serious inroads on the herds. But hunting did little permanent damage to the total elk population, which was nearly wiped out by serious reduction of its winter grazing areas.

Distressed by the pitiful condition of the starving elk, Jackson Hole residents lobbied for the establishment of the National Elk Refuge in 1912. From late November to early May about 60 percent of the Jackson Hole elk herd now finds refuge on this vital winter range. Numbering some 7,500 animals, they constitute one of the world's most impressive wildlife spectacles.

Even the 24,000-acre elk refuge on the edge of Jackson is a much smaller area than these animals once utilized. It would be seriously overgrazed and unable to support the herd if supplemental feeding were not begun midway through the winter. Accustomed to U.S. Fish and Wildlife Service trucks or wagons rolling among them to deliver hay pellets, the elk are not at all concerned when horse-drawn sleighs full of spectators travel through the herd. A close-up view of a bull elk with his magnificent rack of antlers set against a backdrop of the Tetons decked in winter snow is a sight to which few others can compare.

Indeed, there are many incomparable sights in the Tetons — new and completely unique sights created whenever the light changes as the result of a passing cloud or passing season. A mere 9 or 10 million years old, the Tetons are youngsters among mountains and display constantly the vibrancy of their youth. To preserve this vibrant spirit of the mountains, Grand Teton National Park was created in 1929 and expanded in 1950.

The park preserves and displays one of the greatest of America's scenic treasures. But it also distributes this treasure to people who use it to stir their imaginations, to generate gasps of wonder, and to reveal to themselves the truth that fairy-tale beauty has a very real and tangible existence in this world.

Visiting Yellowstone National Park
How To Get There

Yellowstone is located primarily in the northwest corner of Wyoming with parts of the park in Montana and Idaho. By auto, it is 544 miles north of Denver, Colorado, and 320 miles from Salt Lake City, Utah. Airline service is through Jackson, Wyoming; Idaho Falls, Idaho; and Bozeman and Billings, Montana. An airport in West Yellowstone, Montana, operates in summer. Bus lines serve the surrounding towns, and a concessioner provides bus tours through the park in summer and snowcoaches in winter.

Accommodations

There are a wide variety of concessioner-run hotels, lodges, and cabins within the national park. For more information about them, contact TW Services, Yellowstone Park Division, Yellowstone National Park, Wyoming 82190. There is also a complete range of accommodations in surrounding communities. For information about campgrounds within the national park, write to The Superintendent, Yellowstone National Park, Wyoming 82190. There are also campgrounds within the four surrounding national forests.

Activities

Things to do in Yellowstone National Park include hiking the 1000 miles of trails, backpacking, fishing, horseback riding, boating, stage coach riding, picnicking, ski touring, snowmobiling, observing wildlife, and visiting several park museums and visitor centers. The only roads kept open to autos in winter are between Gardiner and Mammoth Hot Springs and from there on to the Northeast Entrance and Cooke City, Montana. The park's interior is accessible in winter by snowmobiles that can be rented nearby or by snowcoaches run by TW Services, Inc.

Special Sights

Old Faithful Geyser is the best known attraction in Yellowstone and justifiably so. Vying with the many geysers and hot springs is the Grand Canyon of the Yellowstone. The mountains along the park's north edge, such as Electric Peak or Barronette and Abiathar peaks, are the most spectacular. A hike to the top of Mount Washburn provides broad views and probable sightings of bighorn sheep. Yellowstone and Lewis lakes supply lovely roadside vistas, and many others can be reached by hiking. Volcanic glass from Obsidian Cliff, between Norris Geyser Basin and Mammoth Hot Springs, was used as a trading item among Indians for centuries before Europeans arrived. In three places, park roads cross the continental divide, which sends water from the southwest corner to the Pacific Ocean, while the rest of the park's streams flow toward the Atlantic.

Yellowstone National Park

National parks began at Yellowstone. In 1870, a group of prominent men in Montana Territory headed south from Helena with a U.S. Cavalry escort to investigate the truth of rumors about a land of stone trees, glass mountains, giant waterfalls, bubbling hot springs, and plumes of steam and water that roared into the sky. Led by Henry D. Washburn, surveyor-general of Montana Territory, the expedition spent several weeks exploring a land that usually wrecked any reputation for truthfulness held by anyone who described the Yellowstone country accurately.

Tradition maintains that, astounded by the bizarre country they were experiencing, the group sat around a campfire near the Madison River below what today is called National Park Mountain. Their talk turned to how enterprising people could stake claim to this wondrous land and grow wealthy exploiting its marvels. Then a nobler thought rose in the light of dancing flames. It was decided that such a land was too fine to be possessed by individuals and that it should be preserved instead in a national park for the benefit of everyone.

The following year, a federal survey team under the leadership of Ferdinand Hayden was motivated by the reports of the Washburn party to investigate the Yellowstone area. With Hayden came frontier photographer William H. Jackson, who documented with indisputable photos the wonders of the world's largest collection of geysers, incredible waterfalls and picturesque canyons, terraced hot springs, and a huge mountain lake. In early 1872, as part of a lobbying effort by national park proponents, these photos were placed on the desks of U.S. Congressmen, who were persuaded to set aside 2.2 million Yellowstone acres as the world's first national park.

In addition to its claim as the first national park in history, Yellowstone may well claim to be one of the best national parks in terms of the wonders it presents. More than 10,000 hot water features, including more than half of the world's geysers, send plumes of steam wafting above the forest of lodgepole pine. Other volcanic landmarks bear witness to the power of the earth's molten mantle just barely contained below a crust that is particularly thin in this place. Alpine peaks carved by glaciers testify that ice can be as powerful and dramatic a shaper of land as can fire. Awesome waterfalls point out the power of erosion to gouge the land through zones of weakness. Layers of petrified trees, stacked standing one above the other, proclaim that life constantly struggles to take over the surface disrupted by inanimate natural power.

But probably most impressive to most visitors are the liv-

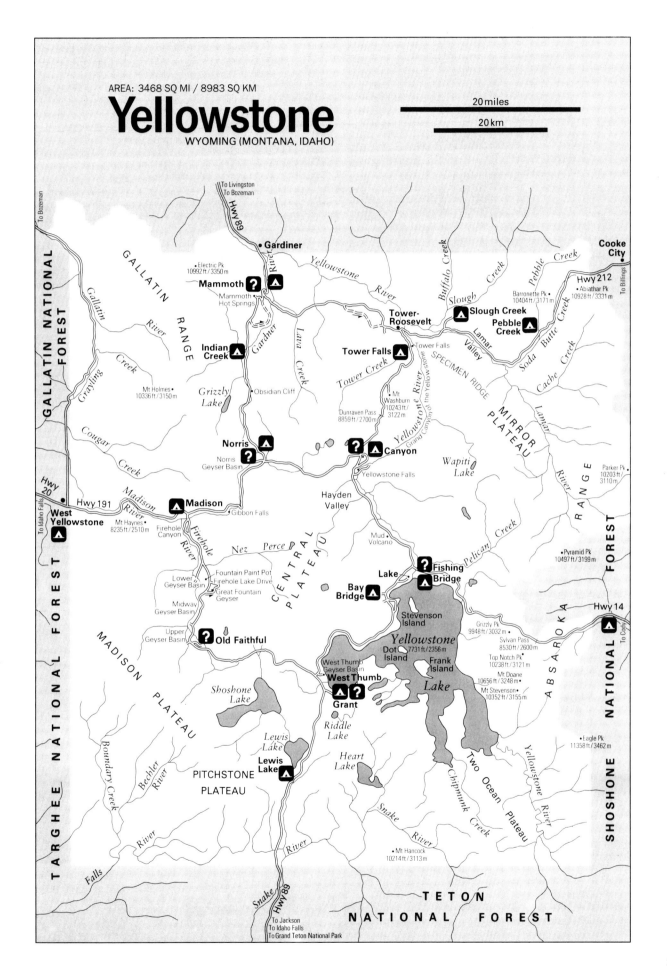

AREA: 3468 SQ MI / 8983 SQ KM

Yellowstone
WYOMING (MONTANA, IDAHO)

20 miles

20 km

ing things that are permitted to dominate Yellowstone today. Nowhere in America is there a better collection of free-roaming wild animals than in Yellowstone National Park. The memory of the bison bull that stood in the path coming back from the hot spring will remain vivid long after the name and appearance of the spring are forgotten.

Elk are the most common of the big mammals that make Yellowstone a mecca for wildlife watchers and photographers. Grouped into five herds, elk are likely to be seen along most park roads in spring, summer, and fall. In winter, many migrate out of the park, but there still remain thousands to be seen along the Northeast Entrance Road. Perhaps even more interesting are those that use the hot water areas along the Firehole River in the park's interior to escape the deep snows that blanket the rest of the park. Other common members of the deer family in Yellowstone are mule deer and moose.

Pronghorn can be seen any time of the year in the northern part of the park. They inhabit the open areas, especially sagebrush flats near Mammoth Hot Springs. In summer, they also migrate into the Lamar Valley along the Northeast Entrance Road.

Bighorn sheep prefer steep, rocky slopes, where their sure-footedness makes them nearly invulnerable to predators. They are easy to spot by hiking up Mount Washburn in summer. In winter, they concentrate on the slopes of Mount Everts between Mammoth Hot Springs and Gardiner, Montana, as well as on the slopes around the Northeast Entrance Road near Tower Junction and near the confluence of Soda Butte Creek and the Lamar River.

Bison comprise one of the great success stories of Yellowstone, for in the national park they received protection while the species was being hunted close to extinction elsewhere. Only in Yellowstone did wild bison survive. These were supplemented by bison from captive herds, and are very common today. They seem especially massive standing out against winter snow in the valleys of the Lamar and Firehole rivers. In the warm weather months, lone bulls may be seen in the Hayden Valley. Close approach to bison should be avoided, for insufficiently cautious visitors have been gored. One man was even killed by a bison that was too closely pressed.

The coyote is the most common predator in Yellowstone National Park. Black bears, which once panhandled along roadsides, have been weaned back to natural foods, which include nearly anything in the woods and meadows. Yellowstone is one of the few hopes left for grizzly bear survival south of Canada. The park and surrounding national forests contain perhaps 200 grizzlies, a quarter of the estimated population in the United States south of Alaska.

Although encountering either bear species is unlikely, hikers on Yellowstone's 1000-mile trail system should be cautious. Making noise while walking is the chief precaution; bears usually avoid humans when they hear us ap-

proach. Another precaution is suspending food in trees away from tents while camping. In case of an accidental encounter, a slow, backwards retreat is the best policy. Adult grizzlies usually cannot climb trees; on the other hand neither can most adult humans, at least not with sufficient speed. Detailed information about safe relations with bears is available at Park Service visitor centers.

Trumpeter swans are another major Yellowstone success story. They were preserved here and at nearby Red Rock Lakes National Wildlife Refuge while being hunted nearly to extinction elsewhere. Now protected, they can be seen on the larger lakes, in potholes in the Lamar Valley, and on the Madison and Yellowstone rivers. Astoundingly graceful and lovely at any time of the year, swans have a mystic quality about them when seen swimming amid mists floating along the Firehole River in winter.

Another large white bird that nests in Yellowstone is the white pelican. It fills its huge bill pouch with cutthroat trout in Yellowstone Lake and along the Yellowstone River.

The osprey, another fish eater, is fairly common in Yellowstone during the warm months. Osprey are particularly impressive when seen from above as they soar between the walls of the Grand Canyon of the Yellowstone. Osprey nest on rocky pinnacles along the canyon walls.

Despite the modern popularity of the park's wildlife, it was in Yellowstone's caldrons of extremely odd geology that the idea for a national park was first cooked up. Yellowstone's geology is based on heat, the internal heat of the earth, which is hot enough to melt rock. In some places beneath the earth's surface, this molten rock – magma – accumulates in chambers. Eventually, the magma in these pools either flows to the surface as volcanic eruptions, where it is called lava, or cools deep below the surface by transmitting its heat to the surrounding solid rock. A mere three to six miles below the surface at Yellowstone, huge reservoirs of semimolten rock are heating up the solid rock around them. Normal thickness of the earth's crust on the continents is between 15 and 30 miles.

Extensively fractured by past volcanic eruptions, the earth's crust in Yellowstone's thermal areas is a net of cracks and crevices. Water percolates down these cracks until it finally reaches the rocks heated by the magma 10 to 14 thousand feet below the surface. The rocks heat the water, making it more capable of dissolving larger passageways along the cracks. Thereby is created what is usually referred to as a plumbing system.

The water closest to the hot rocks has the weight of thousands of feet of water on top of it, exerting great pressure. Water under pressure can be heated to a much higher temperature before turning into steam. However, hot water is less dense than cold and so rises while the cold water sinks to become hot water. As the hot water rises, the pressure on it decreases as less and less water weighs it down. Finally, the pressure is reduced to the point where the superheated water boils. Gradual reduction in pressure permits relatively mild boiling and the creation of normal hot springs.

However, a constriction in the »plumbing« may cause boiling bubbles to block the passage and maintain the pressure on the superhot water below – for a while. Eventually, though, the cork of bubbles is forced out of the way suddenly. Immediately, the pressure is released, and the superhot water »flashes« into steam. The volume of the water is many times greater as steam than as a liquid, and the liquid water remaining on top of the steam is pushed out of the ground with explosive force as the steam bursts into the air. This is a geyser, and Yellowstone has approximately 300 of them.

Some geysers erupt with predictable regularity. The most predictable, and one of the most spectacular of them all, is Old Faithful, symbol of Yellowstone and to some extent of all national parks. Reputed to roar from the ground every hour, the actual interval is 72.7 minutes with extremes between 10 and 120 minutes. Eruption lasts between 1.5 and 5.5 minutes. The geyser shoots its plume of water and steam an average maximum height of 130 feet for about 20 seconds. Devoted geyser gazers recorded Old Faithful's performance so faithfully over the last century that a table was devised whereby the time of the next eruption could be calculated with rough accuracy by measuring the duration of the previous eruption.

Old Faithful puts on such a good show so frequently that it draws hundreds of people to most of its daylight performances during the summer. Nearly everyone goes away from the spectacle believing that it was worth the trouble to see it.

Ironically, Old Faithful and the other hot water features of Yellowstone are at their best when very few people are around – in winter. The contrast and conflict of very hot water with the very cold air of Yellowstone's winter is wondrously impressive. Also in winter, Yellowstone's abundant wild animals congregate near hot water, where they receive respite from deep snow.

The roads are closed by snow, but access is available from near the park boundaries by concessioner-run snow coach – a fairly comfortable vehicle with treads and windows – or by snowmobiles. Some hardy cross-country skiers also make the 50- or 62-mile trip – depending on starting point – to Old Faithful in winter.

Located in the two-square-mile Upper Geyser Basin, Old Faithful is not the only show, nor even necessarily the best one, within this largest concentration of geysers in the national park. Even though most geysers do not erupt as often as remarkable Old Faithful, there are enough of them in the Upper Geyser Basin to guarantee visitors seeing several different performances in an hour.

Each geyser has its own unique charm. Sawmill and Grand are of the type called fountain geysers because they send their water and steam in several directions from a central pool. Old Faithful and Beehive explode through a narrow nozzle, sending their jet skyward. Riverside, which most closely approaches Old Faithful in regularity, blows its water and vapors at an angle over the Firehole River. This river stays ice-free all winter because hot water drains into it from geysers and other hot springs.

Geysers are a special kind of hot springs. Yellowstone has other hot springs that are special for other reasons besides dramatic eruption. In Midway Geyser Basin is Grand Prismatic Spring, the park's largest, with elegant rings of color ranging from deep, dark blue in the center to oranges and yellows on the edges colored by hot water algae. Nearby is the awesome crater of Excelsior Geyser, which erupted in 1985 for the first time since 1890. It discharges 4,000 gallons per minute into the Firehole River, more than any other spring in the park.

Norris Geyser Basin is the hottest and most variable geyser basin in Yellowstone. Very obvious are skeletons of lodgepole pines that grew to maturity here only to be killed by expansion of the hot water's domain. The Norris collection of hot springs, bubbling mud pots, steam vents, and geysers constantly shifts its activity, probably because of blocking of old underground channels and opening of new ones.

Nearly all of Yellowstone's geysers and many of its other hot springs build up thin layers of rock where the water comes to the surface. In the geyser basins, most of the material deposited is called sinter. Sinter is a rock formed by the precipitation of minerals, chiefly silica, picked up by the hot water as it passes through volcanic rock.

Sinter deposits can be very elaborate, such as those at Castle and Grotto geysers. At other places, the deposits may be very thin, forming a solid-looking cover over extremely hot water. Skeletons visible in the bottoms of some hot springs testify to the fact that large mammals occasionally fall through the crusts and are burned to death in the hot water. And it has happened to humans as well.

The National Park Service has tried to make the heavily visited hot water areas safe for the public with boardwalks and railings. Although an intrusion on the naturalness and beauty of the park, these safety features are a necessary compromise and are kept as inconspicuous as possible. But it is neither desirable nor possible to build boardwalks and railings around every potential hazard in the park. Visitors must exhibit a minimum amount of good sense and caution if they are to be safe in Yellowstone.

Mud is deposited around some hot springs, sometimes colored red and yellow by iron oxides, such as at Fountain Paint Pots. At the Mud Volcano hot springs area, natural carbonic and sulfuric acids dissolve the rocks to clay mud but lack enough water to carry off the mud lifted to the surface of the various hot springs. The water is not boiling at the springs' surfaces but bubbles with escaping gases and reeks with the rotten-egg smell of hydrogen sulphide. At Mud Volcano itself, escaping gas propels drops of thick mud five to six feet into the air, which build up a miniature volcano-like crater. Nearby, dramatically named Dragon's Mouth recycles its supply of water, draining it down, only to expel it again with savage vigor.

Mammoth Hot Springs exhibit yet another type of deposit because they discharge a great deal of hot water that first passes through underground chambers of limestone. The hot water dissolves much of this sedimentary rock and deposits it on the surface as travertine – as much as two tons each day.

The depositing of so much travertine causes the terraces of this active spring to change in appearance monthly. The terraces are shaped like giant lily pads, active ones containing shallow pools of water within their turned up edges. The delicate hues of Mammoth Hot Springs are the result of algae growing in water that cools as it flows to lower levels from the pearly white source in the upper terraces, where the water is still too hot to support algae.

Soda Butte is an isolated hot water feature along the Northeast Entrance Road formed by the same process that created Mammoth Hot Springs' terraces. Hot water carried a load of dissolved limestone to the surface and deposited it when carbon dioxide in the water escaped to the atmosphere. Because water no longer flows actively from Soda Butte, it stands as a dull gray cone immediately south of the road. Without a constant supply of hot water, the algae that color such features die, and the rock dries out to its normal drab color.

Hot water is responsible for Yellowstone National Park's other great geological features besides its hot springs. The grandeur of Grand Canyon of the Yellowstone may be equalled, but is not surpassed, by any other canyon on earth. Twenty miles long and 1,500 feet deep in places, the canyon is strikingly V-shaped. Its yellow, gold, pink, and brown walls drop steeply to a whitewater river that plunges into the canyon in waterfalls of great size and beauty. Goblinlike hoodoos, rough rock columns, accent the walls below the many viewing points along the rim.

All this wonder is possible because the weak volcanic rock through which the Yellowstone River cuts has been decomposed by hot water and volcanic fumes. The remarkable color of the rock is the result of the alteration of iron minerals by the fumes. An extra touch of fantasy is added by steam rising from vents and hot springs deep within the canyon.

The magnificent Lower Falls of the Yellowstone River plunge 308 feet into the canyon over a lip of harder volcanic rock that has not been altered by exposure to hot water and decomposing fumes. This barrier to erosion by the river has caused the canyon to deepen much faster below the barrier than above it. A differing rate of erosion causes the huge step over which the river falls.

With all its frothing, roaring, bubbling, steaming, splashing, and flowing, Yellowstone geology seems remarkably active and unstable. However, the present is a relatively peaceful, quiet time in the violent history of this unstable landscape.

The story started some 2.7 billion years ago with compression and recrystallization of sedimentary or volcanic rock into metamorphic rock, gneiss and schist, which underlies most of North America. Things began to get active about 600 million years ago as shallow seas spread broadly over this area at least a dozen times. Thick sheets of sandy and limy rock were laid down in this aquatic environment.

Approximately 75 million years ago, a mountain-building warp of the earth's crust lifted and broke these layers. Arches rose in the surface, then were pushed over each other until ancient metamorphic rocks in some places lay on top of much younger sedimentary rocks. Meanwhile, erosion carried away sedimentary layers from the highest parts of the arches and revealed the harder metamorphics below.

As if this unorderly jumble of rocks was not already thoroughly mixed, about 50 million years ago began a violent volcanic time. Lava flowed all over the land, layered with volcanic ash, broken rock, and dust.

During centuries between these eruptions, forests typical of a temperate climate – such as North Carolina's – covered the landscape. Wide-scale uplift of the land had not yet occurred, and the climate was that of an elevation of only 2,000 feet. After each forest regrew, volcanoes would erupt again, killing the trees, burying some in mudflows where they stood or flooding them in ponds dammed by mudflows. Other trees were transported by mudflows and deposited in upright or horizontal positions. Layers of different stone forests destroyed by successive volcanic episodes sit atop each other in Specimen Ridge above the Lamar Valley.

The buried wood later petrified as groundwater that passed through volcanic rock deposited dissolved silica in place of the organic material in the trees, preserving their tiniest features in stone. Stone forests atop Specimen Ridge are camouflaged by living forests, for the standing, branchless petrified trunks look much like stumps of modern trees from a short distance away. The stone stumps atop Specimen Ridge can be reached only by hiking. They can be picked out with binoculars and persistence by focusing on the ridge top south of the Northeast Entrance Road about five miles east of Tower Junction.

Of course, no specimens of petrified wood or anything else should be collected from a national park. The only standing petrified tree in Yellowstone near a road is not surrounded by a living forest. It stands alone surrounded by a fence. The fence is present because three petrified trees once stood on this slope reached by a well-marked road 16 miles east of Mammoth Hot Springs. The other stone trees were carried away piece by piece.

The volcanoes quieted down about 38 million years ago and the entire area was uplifted some 5,000 to 6,000 feet beginning about 12 million years ago. The details of whatever mountains were built by this uplift were destroyed when Yellowstone exploded.

An extremely large magma chamber evidently formed and pushed upward in a blister that ruptured volcanic rock on the surface. But for a long time, only a little magma and gas escaped to the surface through a circle of breaks around the edge of the blister above the chamber. The rest of the huge bulk of magma and volcanic gas was held under great pressure beneath the surface.

Then, about 2 million years ago, more gas and magma began to escape. This slight lessening of pressure permitted the volcanic gases in the magma chamber to expand suddenly and blow out through the circle of breaks in a gigantic explosion. In a flash of incomprehensibly great destruction, most of the previously existing Yellowstone volcanoes were obliterated as 600 cubic miles of volcanic debris roared into the atmosphere, some spreading as far away as Saskatchewan and Texas. Twelve hundred square miles of the present national park were completely obliterated.

After all that subterranean rock blew out, the roof of the magma chamber collapsed into the space it had occupied. The resulting giant hole, or caldera, extends out of the park into Idaho.

And then it all happened again around 1.2 million years ago, creating a newer, smaller caldera within the Idaho portion of the older one. More eruptions followed within today's national park. Two more magma chambers formed that exploded with double-barreled impact about 600,000 years ago. After the magma exploded out of these chambers, they too collapsed, forming a caldera. Yellowstone Lake, the largest lake in North America at so high an altitude (7,731 feet), occupies part of this caldera. Some of the rest has been covered by later lava flows. The West Thumb bay of Yellowstone Lake formed between 200,000 and 125,000 years ago after the collapse of yet another magma chamber roof that followed a smaller blowout of lava and gas.

These later flows and magma chamber explosions came into conflict with masses of glacial ice that covered most of the park. Where molten rock and rivers of ice met, the effects of their conflicting powers must have been so enormous that the conflicts between today's hot geyser basins and winter cold seem tame by comparison. Each advance of the glaciers smoothed down the land and sculpted the peaks. Boulders of metamorphic rock rode within and on the rivers of ice to be dropped atop volcanic flows many miles from where the boulders had been quarried by the glaciers.

Ice or debris dropped when the ice melted and dammed rivers, forming broad lakes. Silt that accumulated in the lakes now supports lush pasture for wildlife. The Hayden Valley, with its population of bison, moose, and elk, is such a former lake bed. The last ice sheet retreated only 8,500 years ago.

Yellowstone's most spectacular glacier-carved peaks decorate its northern edge. However, a closer view of the sculpturing of mountains by ice can be had along one of America's most scenic highways, beyond the border of the national park. From the Northeast Entrance, the Beartooth Highway climbs above tree line and winds over alpine tundra amid dramatic glaciated peaks before dropping through hairpin switchbacks to Red Lodge, Montana. Driving this road, although it is not within the park, will add even more variety to the already extremely varied Yellowstone experience.

Through open places in the subalpine forest east of Cooke City, motorists can spot pointed Pilot Peak and ragged-topped Index Peak rising above the water-deposited gravel along Clarks Fork of the Yellowstone River. These landmark summits tower on the northeast edge of North Absaroka Wilderness Area. Pilot at 11,708 feet is 395 feet higher than Index. Both are glaciated remnants of a great volcano crater. Index once filled the crater; Pilot was part of a lava flow on the crater wall.

The vistas open up when the forest becomes less dense as the road climbs the Beartooth Plateau. At Beartooth Lake, motorists can look 1000 feet up to the cliffs of Beartooth Butte and see a patch of red rock. This is compacted mud and sand that was laid down in an ancient stream. The red rock's fossils are plants and primitive armor-plated fish. The surrounding rock was laid down in an ocean about 400 million years ago and contains marine fossils such as trilobites, crinoids, brachiopods, and corals.

Beartooth is the first of many lakes that line the highway. Next is Island Lake, a campground site at the end of a short spur road to the north. Left by retreating glaciers, lakes beyond Island seem numberless as they spangle the grassy tundra tableland viewed from switchbacks below Beartooth Pass. The pass is the highest point on the road, 10,940 feet above sea level.

Ranks of glacier-carved peaks spread a jagged vista north of the road in the vicinity of the pass. Sharpest of all is the Beartooth for which so many features in the area are named. East of the pass are fine views of Cirque Lake, appropriately named for the basin in which it sits, a rock-walled amphitheater plucked from the headwall of a glacier. Far below, Rock Creek Valley displays the classic U-shape of a glaciated valley.

It is assumed that the present time is only a warm period between advances of glacial ice. Also, layers of petrified forests in Specimen Ridge indicate that there have been centuries of calm between periods of volcanic catastrophe.

The center of Yellowstone National Park seems to be bulging upward a little every year. Instruments at the Old Faithful Visitor Center record as many as 100 small earthquakes daily. Major quakes hit the park and disrupted many of its hot water features in 1959, 1975, and 1983. In steamy, bubbling, vibrant Yellowstone, change, either subtle or dramatic, is ever-present.

Visiting Glacier And Waterton Lakes National Parks

How To Get There

Airlines serve Great Falls, Montana (143 miles southeast), Kalispell, Montana (32 miles southwest), Lethbridge, Alberta (80 miles northeast), and Pincher Creek, Alberta (34 miles north). Amtrak brings railroad passengers to West Glacier and East Glacier Park, both just outside national park boundaries. Bus service connects the parks with Great Falls and Pincher Creek. But a very large majority of park visitors arrive by private automobile.

Accommodations

Glacier and Waterton Lakes national parks boast attractive hotels of genuine historic significance. In addition to these concessioner-operated facilities within the parks, there are a wide range of lodges, motels, and cabins outside Glacier's park boundaries, and in Waterton Park. The National Park Service also operates several campgrounds within Glacier. For more information, write to The Superintendent, Glacier National Park, West Glacier, Montana 59936. Information about lodging in Waterton can be obtained from The Superintendent, Waterton Lakes National Park, Waterton Park, Alberta TOK 2MO.

Activities

Things to do in Glacier and Waterton Lakes national parks include hiking the more than 850-mile trail systems in both parks, backpacking, fishing, horseback riding, boat cruises, canoeing, picnicking, cross-country skiing, observing wildlife, and driving very scenic park roads. Going-to-the-Sun Road, which climbs to an elevation of 6,680 feet at Logan Pass, normally is open in winter only for the 10 miles between West Glacier and Lake McDonald Lodge. Chief Mountain International Highway is usually closed from mid-September to mid-May.

Special Sights

Spectacular vistas in Glacier include Lake McDonald, St. Mary Lake and Wild Goose Island, Swiftcurrent Lake, Two Medicine Lake and Running Eagle Falls, Logan Pass, and the Highline Trail to Granite Park. Not to be missed in Waterton Lakes National Park are Cameron Falls, Cameron Lake, and the nature trail to Blakiston Falls from Red Rock Warden Station.

These two parks were united, at the urging of many people, as »Waterton/Glacier International Peace Park« in 1932, and this land of natural splendors is dedicated to peace and to an international friendship that has few rivals.

Glacier National Park

About 50 glaciers deck the peaks of Glacier National Park. But the count was 90 when the park was created in 1910. The twentieth century has been a time of retreat for the glaciers of this national park. But their much larger predecessors between 10,000 and 6,000 years ago carved the signs of glaciation all across these mountains.

Mountain glaciers shaped Glacier National Park in basically the same way as they carved the other national parks of the Rocky Mountains. The final product looks somewhat different in Glacier, though, because Glacier's rocks differ significantly from those that create the great glacial vistas in Rocky Mountain and Grand Teton national parks. The mountains of Glacier are built of sedimentary rock, some of the oldest sedimentary rock in the world. The layered look of the sedimentary rock gives these mountains a distinctive character, easy to distinguish from the igneous and metamorphic peaks further south.

A particularly lovely aspect of Glacier National Park is the color of red and gray-green strata of ancient sedimentary rocks that ribbon its mountainsides. More colors, festive red and green, water-rounded cobbles, pave its lakeshores and streambeds. It was about a billion years ago that these rocks were laid down as mud, silt, and sand. In most rocks of this ancient age, heat and pressure over many eons have so changed their appearance that very little can be determined about their origins. But the rocks of Glacier have retained such details as the tiny craters made by raindrops that fell before there were plants on the land to shield it from the erosion of moving water. The ridges shaped by waves and currents in mud many millions of years ago look so fresh that a hiker might try to step over the now solid rock in which they occur, thinking that it looks like fresh mud. Mudcracks in other layers reveal a drying of the ground long ages past. Even the colors of the rocks hold clues about the environment in which these layers first came to rest.

Today Glacier National Park boasts an incredible display of wild plants and animals. Less attention-grabbing, but also interesting, are the park's fossils of some of the oldest living things. Called stromatolites, these fossils, described as looking like cabbages, are the imprint of blue-green algae, most primitive of seaweeds. A scummy flotsam on ocean waves, they do not look very impressive either alive or as fossils, but their conversion of carbon dioxide to free oxygen has given us a breathable atmosphere.

Erosion was tearing down most of the world between 1 billion and 600 million years ago. Most of North America was flattened to a featureless plain. A good deal of silt, sand, and mud – the debris of erosion – accumulated in today's Glacier National Park. Some was laid down on ocean floors, forming rocks today called Altyn and Siyeh

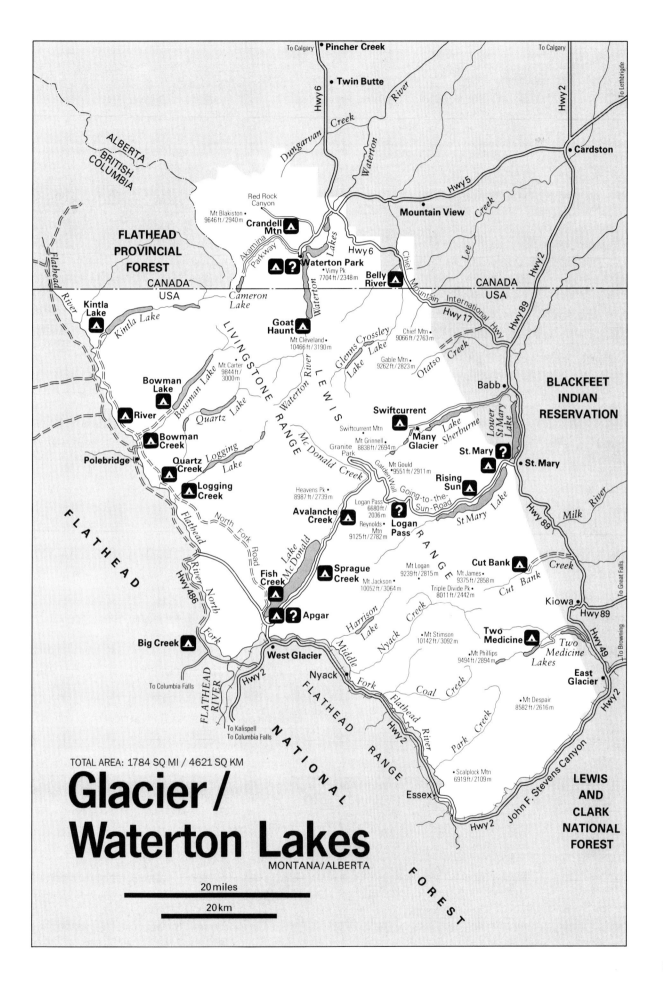

Glacier / Waterton Lakes

MONTANA/ALBERTA

TOTAL AREA: 1784 SQ MI / 4621 SQ KM

20 miles

20 km

limestones. Colorful Appekunny and Grinnell formations came to be in areas that alternated between wet and dry – river floodplains or tide flats.

Then, 1,080 million years ago – as revealed by dating of radioactive minerals naturally occurring in the rocks – molten rock carrying a dark load of iron rose from deep within the earth to force its way through the sedimentary rocks. Where it spread horizontally through limestone, the liquid rock's heat changed the surrounding rock into marble. Today a very prominent dark line in the mountain walls, called the Purcell sill, is this cooled igneous rock set off above and below by layers of white marble.

Later eruptions of lava came to the surface under ocean waters and immediately cooled to a fine-grained rock called basalt. One of Glacier's most popular hiking destinations, Granite Park, was named for the basalt seen there. When the area was named, the basalt was mistaken for granite, which is not found on the surface of this national park.

For hundreds of millions of years after the ancient sedimentary rocks were formed, seas advanced and retreated. Life evolved more complicated forms that left their traces in subsequent layers of sedimentary rock. Erosion stripped much of this rock away until the oceans returned and more layers of mud and silt were deposited. Between 100 and 70 million years ago, these deposits formed deep beds of clay that were eventually compressed to shale. These layers were destined to be very important in the development of Glacier's mountains.

During the Laramide Orogeny caused by the splitting of North America from Europe some 70 million years ago, the Rocky Mountain chain was uplifted. The earth's crust warped up and tilted eastward the flat-lying rock layers west of Glacier National Park. An incredibly huge block of sedimentary rock – 75 by 19 miles – began sliding east, downhill over what is called the Lewis Overthrust Fault. This gradual slide was lubricated by the layers of clay-shale and permitted rock layers that were very ancient to ride over layers that were many millions of years younger. Thus older rocks that were laid down first ended up on top of younger rocks that were deposited later, quite different from the normal sequence of youngest rocks on top. This slide of a huge block of the earth's crust covered about 40 miles. Today it makes up the Lewis and Livingstone Ranges in Glacier National Park. The very lovely Flathead Valley, through which many visitors approach the national park from the west, was formed in part in the gap left behind when the mountain block slid east.

What goes up, it is said, must come down. And erosion began tearing down the new mountains even as they were lifted up. The shale that sat on top of the old rocks and made the lubricating layer just below them was washed away from the top. Then the forces of weathering began to eat into the ancient rocks, filling the valleys with colorful sediments, almost burying the mountains in aprons of debris.

But more uplift occurred some 10 million years ago, and greater elevation created a cooler, wetter climate. Not only was there more precipitation, but the uplift also gave that extra water more power to carry away more sediments and reveal the buried mountains.

An increase in precipitation, perhaps coupled with a lowering of average temperature, introduced the Ice Ages to North America about 3 million years ago. Continental ice sheets advanced across the land. But the main mountain glaciers that originated high on the slopes and flowed down river-cut valleys seem to have had their greatest effect during the last 200,000 years.

During this time, three periods of glacial advances sculpted the peaks of Glacier National Park. Valleys were deepened and their sides steepened. Troughs scooped in the valley floors were dammed by walls of rock and dirt – moraines – dropped by the glaciers. Water empounded behind these moraines and contained within troughs are the many finger lakes, such as St. Mary Lake and Lake McDonald, that charm millions of park visitors.

Near the summits, so many glaciers scooped cirques from their headwalls that very little was left of the peak tops, leaving them very pointed and steep. The Garden Wall, which rises between Lake McDonald and the Many Glacier area, is a high ridge attacked by glacial ice on both sides. In places it is only a few yards wide at the top, and windows pierce all the way through the thin wall.

The last of the mountain-shaping ice disappeared completely in a warm period about 6,000 years ago. Modern glaciers came to be as the climate cooled again approximately 3,000 years ago.

When the glaciers melted, they left behind a sharpened landscape marked by an invisible, but very influential, line running along some of the highest ridgetops, including the Garden Wall, approximately north to south through the park. This is the continental divide, which separates waters flowing toward either the Atlantic or the Pacific oceans.

But in Glacier, on the summit of Triple Divide Mountain, the continental divide meets the Hudson Bay divide. Water from this point flows not only to the Pacific by way of the Columbia River system and to the Atlantic by way of the Mississippi, but also north into Hudson Bay via the Saskatchewan River.

The continental divide is more than a geographic curiosity in the national park. It is also the dividing line between two types of climate. The west side of Glacier is dominated by the damp Pacific Northwest weather, averaging 28 inches of moisture each year.

Sheltered in steep-walled valleys from icy Canadian air that sweeps down on the east slope of the park, the west or wet side of Glacier is overcast much of the time. The cloud cover holds the day's heat close to the earth. Without the clouds, warmth would radiate into clear skies. The forests nourished by this abundance of water and relatively mild climate are lush, home to massive western red cedar, western hemlock, and black cottonwood. Here, too, live white-tailed deer, which, unlike the more common mule deer, are not found in the other national parks of the Rockies.

As the weather systems move east, they strike the high peaks and ridges of the continental divide. Moisture is stripped from the clouds and little is left for the east side of the divide, where average precipitation is only 18 inches per year. Motorists crossing the park on Going-to-the-Sun Road see at once what 10 inches less per year means. The forests east of Logan Pass are much less dense and lack the primeval mood of the forests on the park's west side.

Going-to-the-Sun Road reveals climatic changes that occur not only on opposite sides of the mountains but also at different elevations. Because average temperature drops with gain in altitude while precipitation, wind speed, and evaporation increase, different plant species grow more successfully at different elevations. Northern or southern exposure, steepness of slope, type of soil, and forest fire are other factors that complicate an otherwise orderly stratification of plant zones on the mountainsides.

From bits of treeless prairie that extend a short way into the park as far as St. Mary Lake on the east slope, the road climbs into the coniferous forest. Here Douglas-fir, lodgepole pine, and western larch grow rather widely spaced, together with Engelmann spruce and subalpine fir. Higher still, the climate becomes less suitable for tree survival; Engelmann spruce, subalpine fir, and whitebark pine assume a stunted posture, pruned, battered, and blasted by the wind.

In the vicinity of Logan Pass, the road rises above tree line. Here only ground-hugging plants, such as grasses and wildflowers, can survive the harsh weather. But in summer these put on a beautiful display of color.

Some flowers grow throughout the plant zones, from the lowest levels of the park to tree line, but bloom at different times during the summer. Beargrass, a large and striking cream-colored member of the lily family, begins blooming in spring at lower elevations. As the season progresses, fields of blooming beargrass unfold at constantly higher elevations until this flower colors the wake of melting tree line snowbanks in September.

Many park visitors experience the impressive display of tundra wildflowers by hiking along the easy trail from Logan Pass to an overlook of Hidden Lake. A boardwalk has been constructed from the visitor center at the pass up through abundant flowers in the Hanging Gardens area below Reynolds Mountain on the left and Clements Mountain on the right. The elevated walkway protects the surrounding plants from foot traffic.

Besides wildflowers, this trail offers extremely clear examples of the geological phenomena typical of Glacier National Park. Various levels of sedimentary and igneous rocks are distinguished by their colors and obvious layering. Stromatolite heads, the ancient fossils of blue-green algae colonies, are strewn along the trail together with billion-year-old mud cracks and ripple marks.

Even clearer are the surrounding signs of glacial action. Reynolds Mountain is a horn, a peak carved to a dramatic pyramid by glaciers eating away on three sides. »Hanging« valleys show where smaller glaciers could not cut down as fast as more massive ice rivers. The valleys which contained these tributary glaciers thus were left hanging high above the deeper main valleys, into which waterfalls often drop for hundreds of feet.

A small glacier on the side of Clements melted so much within the last few decades that now it is only a permanent icefield. Bodies of ice that are large enough for the ice at the bottom to be so compressed as to flow like liquid plastic are glaciers. If the ice is not sufficiently thick so that its weight causes internal flowing, it is called a permanent icefield. Permanent is a relative term, for the ice may melt away entirely or increase in size to glacial status, depending on whether it collects more snow in winter than can melt in summer. A barren ridge of unsorted loose rock below the icefield on Clements is a terminal moraine, marking the furthest extent of the former glacier.

From the Hidden Lake overlook, hikers gaze down on a typical glacial lake, sitting in a cirque carved by a glacier plucking rock to form a bowl-shaped array of cliffs at its headwall. In the distance, part of Sperry Glacier on Gunsight Mountain appears over a ridge.

On the way to the overlook, walkers may spot mountain goat. Despite being large – about 3.5 feet tall, up to 300 pounds – and conspicuous – shaggy, white coat stands out from rocky or green background –, mountain goats have a remarkable ability to appear from nowhere. If they decide to make an appearance, they likely will be friendly and perhaps as curious about the hikers as the hikers are about mountain goats. With feet made to cling to rocks in unbelievably precipitous places, mountain goats have little to fear from predators, although a golden eagle may try to knock a kid off a cliff. Their sharp, dark horns are used more frequently on other goats than on predators. Besides appearing on cliffs around Going-to-the-Sun Road, mountain goats frequently visit clay cliffs called »The Goat Lick« along Highway 2 on the south edge of the park. They eat minerals in the clay. Of the four national parks of the American Rockies, only Glacier is home to the mountain goat.

Bear or mule deer may also be seen from the Hidden Lake trail. Bighorn sheep sometimes put in an appearance, and hoary marmots and Columbian ground squirrels are common. The camouflage of the white-tailed ptarmigan, a small, alpine grouse, is so perfect that hikers often walk past the bird, believing it to be a lichen-covered rock.

West of Logan Pass, Going-to-the-Sun Road drops past many scenic turnouts, cutting below the Garden Wall cliffs to a young forest of lodgepole pine that grew up after a 1936 forest fire. Then the road makes a sharp hairpin curve to the site of a 1967 forest fire. Skeletons of burned trees line the road, and new growth of deciduous shrubs and trees is coming in thickly. They give the 3109-acre burn a light green color that contrasts with the dark of the surrounding conifers. Probably the next stage of plant succession will be lodgepole that will make the site of the 1967 fire look the same as the present appearance of the 1936 fire zone.

Other zones of disruption can be picked out from the road by their light green deciduous color. Some of these are avalanche chutes, caused when snow cornices deposited by winter winds no longer could resist the pull of gravity and broke off from the ridgetops. Riding a cushion of air trapped beneath many tons of snow, an avalanche falls as fast as 150 miles per hour, destroying all before it.

Landslide scars are also light green, but usually come about from a slow downhill creep rather than an all-consuming rush of mud. Landslides occur when unstable soil is supersaturated by rain and begins to slip downhill. Most of this unstable soil was deposited by conveyor belts of glacial ice confined within the valley walls. When the ice melted, the unsupported soil was left plastered to the bedrock. Since the glaciers melted, most of this unstable glacial till has already responded to the pull of gravity. Hummocky piles of soil at the base of concave scars indicate such slides.

Descending through Engelmann spruce and subalpine fir, the road enters a western red cedar-hemlock forest which many visitors find to be the most enjoyable environment in Glacier National Park. These stately trees, draped with light green goatsbeard lichen, constitute the easternmost extension of the Pacific Coast plant community. Underneath the almost unbroken forest canopy, the light is a dim green, reducing the number of bushes and creating an open setting like the interior of a many-pillared cathedral.

Set in the midst of this forest is Avalanche Campground, at the mouth of Avalanche Creek, which flows from Avalanche Lake into McDonald Creek. There are so many notable features in this park that one name sometimes has to serve many uses. The waters of Avalanche Creek are fed by melting ice from Sperry Glacier. Glacially pulverized rock flour is suspended in the water, coloring it various hues of green according to how much powdered rock the glacier is releasing above. From the campground, a relatively easy and extremely popular trail leads two miles up to Avalanche Lake.

Less than three miles down the road from Avalanche Campground is »Moose Country.« Here McDonald Creek once flowed over sand and gravel washed out of a now-melted glacier. In this easily eroded till, the course of the creek is not confined, and its channel meanders along the nearly level valley floor. Old bends at Moose Country were cut off and isolated to become oxbow ponds that eventually filled in to become swamps. This habitat is ideal for moose and beaver.

A mile below the abandoned channels of Moose Country, McDonald Creek passes over green Appekunny mudstone instead of loose glacial till. Here at McDonald Falls, the creek has cut a channel in this ancient bedrock since the melting of the last big glacier. Torrents of water flowing from the retreating glacier were much heavier than the present flow and probably did most of the cutting of this course, which now holds the creek in place.

The western end of Going-to-the-Sun Road follows Lake McDonald for nine miles, offering many opportunities for scenic views framed by the red cedar-hemlock forest. Surrounding mountains are reflected in the largest of the park's lakes. Red and green cobbles of ancient rock rolled smooth by flowing water color the lake bed.

The outlet of Lake McDonald provides an ideal spawning site for kokanee salmon, planted in Flathead Lake 60 miles south of Glacier in 1916 and multiplied very successfully. Each October into December as thousands of salmon arrive here in McDonald Creek, more than 600 bald eagles have congregated to partake in this bounty – an extremely unusual wildlife spectacle.

The mountains which separate the lush red cedar-hemlock forest from the more austere environment of the east side of the park also served as barriers between warring Indian tribes in the 1700's. Riding horses and carrying guns introduced by white culture, Blackfeet Indians hunted bison on the plains east of today's park. They jealously guarded this rich hunting ground from other tribes such as the Kalispel, Kutenai, and Flathead, who were bottled up on the west side of the mountains, hunting smaller animals and gathering roots and berries.

Blackfeet power faded in the later 1800's, and white explorers, trappers, and prospectors were able to penetrate the mountains that would become Glacier National Park. Hoping to duplicate the rich mineral strikes of the southern Rockies, prospectors were disappointed that these sedimentary rocks offered fewer opportunities to find subterranean treasure. However, before the lack of exploitable minerals was realized, mining interests arranged for the federal government to negotiate sale by the Blackfeet of the mountains east of the continental divide for $1.5 million. Indians of the west slope had already vacated those lands.

When the Great Northern Railroad laid tracks along the southern boundary of today's park, its beauty was soon discovered by the general public. The railroad saw an opportunity to generate passenger traffic from tourists. The idea of a national park in this remote area with little other economic potential created little controversy. Congress established Glacier National Park on May 11, 1910.

Railroad interests built hotels, camps, and rustic chalets in Glacier's wilderness to house the tourists who arrived by rail. Trails were built to bring the tourists from the railroad to the lodging facilities. These trails are the basis of Glacier's present 750-mile trail system. Beginning in

1917, the National Park Service formed plans to build the Going-to-the-Sun Road. Completed in 1932, this 50-mile route across the mountains made the automobile the prime means for viewing the park.

Waterton Lakes National Park

Named for the Upper, Middle, and Lower Waterton lakes which glisten in the central valley of this 200-square-mile park, Waterton Lakes National Park was set aside in 1895. Its chief promoter for park status was John George »Kootenai« Brown, the area's first permanent white resident, whose grave is located near Lower Waterton Lake. The center of activity is Waterton Park townsite, which sits on a delta of glacial sand and rock deposited by meltwater flowing down the Cameron Valley. About 50 miles of park roads wind among a great deal of spectacular scenery jammed into a relatively small area.

One of the most popular of Waterton's drives is the 10-mile-long Akamina Parkway, which follows Cameron Creek up to Cameron Lake. The road passes attractive waterfalls, penetrates a picturesque canyon, and offers the chance of sighting wildlife, such as bighorn sheep. Less than six miles from the townsite at Lineham Brook is the spot where Alberta's first oil well was drilled in 1886. A town to be called Oil City was planned for this site but never was built. The Forty-ninth Parallel, the U.S.-Canada border, cuts across the upper end of Cameron Lake, tucked into a basin below the continental divide.

Red Rock Canyon Road branches from Alberta Highway 5 near a golf course within the park, a little over a mile north of the resplendent Prince of Wales Hotel. Following a former Hudson's Bay Company trail through the mountains, this 9-mile drive provides good views of the ragged turrets of Mount Blakiston, at 9,646 feet the tallest peak in Waterton Lakes National Park. The road also leads to trailheads of many fine hiking paths.

To encounter real wilderness adventure, visitors may also hike into Waterton's high country where only primitive camping facilities are available. This style of camping can be enjoyed in such alpine areas as Crypt Lake, Alderson Lake, Row Lakes, and Twin Lakes.

The Chief Mountain International Highway is the main road that connects Waterton Lakes and Glacier national parks. Winter snows usually close the highway between mid-September and mid-May. From the Montana plains at Babb, the road climbs aspen- and lodgepole-covered hills below Chief Mountain. This isolated, buff-colored tower of limestone is 9,066 feet in elevation. Also majestic are views of Mount Cleveland (10,466 feet), highest peak in Glacier National Park.

North of the International Boundary, marked by customs offices and a broad swath cut through the forest, the Chief Mountain International Highway crosses the Belly River Valley and climbs a forested ridge to Big Bend Over-look. Here the Waterton Valley spreads out in a grand panorama of lakes and peaks.

A most comfortable way to view the mountains and mountain ranges around Waterton Lakes is to enter one of the sightseeing boats at Waterton Park, which cruises across the U.S.-Canada border to the southern end of Upper Waterton Lake in Glacier Park and offers spectacular mountain scenery and lessons about the exciting natural history of the area.

The geology, plants, and animals of Waterton Lakes National Park differ little from those of Glacier, except for the fact that Waterton Lakes is located entirely east of the continental divide. The Waterton dolomite, well exposed at Cameron Falls near Waterton Park townsite, is even older than the oldest rocks visible south of the boundary.

Bison are kept in a drive-through enclosure just off Alberta Highway 6 at the north edge of the park as a reminder of the huge herds that once roamed this area.

Trails, lakes, and streams pass between the two parks with little recognition of international boundaries.

Picture Contents